Joan –

Thank you for presenting me with a Quilt of Honor. I truly appreciate it.

This is the story of my life.

A little Americana

A little history

A little about life — as seen through my eyes.

Please enjoy.

Dave Carden
Sergeant Major
U.S. Army
Special Forces
(Retired)

THE
ARMY
INSIDER

Up Close and Personal

Sergeant Major
David C. Carden
United States Army (Retired)

authorHOUSE

AuthorHouse™
1663 Liberty Drive
Bloomington, IN 47403
www.authorhouse.com
Phone: 833-262-8899

Published by AuthorHouse 11/12/2021

ISBN: 978-1-4490-2048-4 (e)
ISBN: 978-1-4490-2049-1 (sc)
ISBN: 978-1-4490-2050-7 (hc)

Library of Congress Control Number: 2009908615

Print information available on the last page.

Any people depicted in stock imagery provided by Getty Images are models, and such images are being used for illustrative purposes only. Certain stock imagery © Getty Images.

This book is printed on acid-free paper.

Because of the dynamic nature of the Internet, any web addresses or links contained in this book may have changed since publication and may no longer be valid. The views expressed in this work are solely those of the author and do not necessarily reflect the views of the publisher, and the publisher hereby disclaims any responsibility for them.

CONTENTS

Contents

ACKNOWLEDGEMENTS

This is the story of my life. It wouldn't have become a record for future generations without the support, prodding and sometimes cajoling of my family, colleagues and friends. When I was a First Sergeant, and later a Sergeant Major, fellow soldiers of all ranks kept asking me why I hadn't written my memoirs. Honestly, I didn't think I had really accomplished anything. I was fortunate to serve my country and that's all I had ever wanted to do. There are people whom I think have contributed much more than I and some of them mentored me.

I belong to a work and social world-wide online network named Blue Shirt Nation. I joined the group a year after its inception three years ago and made many online friends. Blue Shirt Nation membership is comprised of corporate executives and employees; and the rank and file who are employed in retail, service and support facilities in the United States, Puerto Rico, Mexico, Canada and China. I wrote a few short stories about my life experiences and people expressed an interest in reading more. I discussed this with family and friends and they felt I should write a book as suggested by my online friends.

So thanks are in order. First, I want to thank my Mother and Father because they instilled in me my value system. Also, I want to further thank my Mother for the historical information she provided regarding my ancestors, her early life experience and my Father's early life experience. I received from my parents the determination to succeed and the perseverance to see things through to the end.

Next are my online friends: Jim Boushee, 'theplumber' was the first to say, "DAVID, WRITE YOUR BOOK." Jim has also become an advisor and a close personal friend. Jim Waddick, 'jameswaddick' gave me valuable assistance for titling my stories and the book title itself. Howard Collins, 'howardcollins' came out of nowhere and created a picture story from one of my stories that was the funniest thing ever published on Blue Shirt Nation. Howard provided the inspiration to keep writing. Kam Miller, 'Kam' offered much needed advice and assistance. Kam is a real writer and is currently working on a movie script. Rebecca Kay, 'Rebecca_Kay' impresses me every day with her passion for life, family and work, even in the face of adversity. Keith Syvinski, 'LeoSynapse' is another who provided inspiration. Keith is a professional photographer and his works are copy written under the pseudo name 'LeoSynapse.' Until he told me otherwise, for a long time I thought Keith's real name was Leo Synapse.

Throughout this process, I have many other Blue Shirt Nation friends who provided encouragement. The most vocal are:

> Gary Koelling, 'Gary'
> Steve Bendt, 'Steve'
> Cameron Gross, 'CamG'
> Adam Mulder, 'mulderaj'
> Carissa Partheymueller, 'Applemuffin'
> Christopher Stark, 'ChrisStark'
> Bob Debellis, 'theapplianceman'
> Nicholas Pfeifer, 'TFX'
> David Overton, 'AGiganticPanda'
> Anthony Di Rocco, 'Ajd187'
> Gary Alexander, 'MediaMaster'
> Coral Biegler, 'Coral'
> Stacy Archibald, 'CanAlien3'
> Greg Macfatridge, 'Mcfatty'
> Anthony Zambito, 'desperado'

Next, I want to thank my oldest son Matthew. Two years ago he developed three websites for this book. Now they'll be put to use. I want to thank all my children...Matthew, Steven, Dominic and Catherine...for their support and encouragement.

I want to also thank Janice Glassman. Ms. Glassman is a customer service representative for a major credit card. My credit card. She showed me how to gain immediate access to my funds after I was told by two other people I had to wait 10 days because it was policy and in the fine print of my contract. I am indebted to her and Ms. Glassman is an asset to her financial institution.

Next, my thanks go to Janet Bousquet. She provided much needed technical computer expertise.

I want to thank Mary Linda Baker for brainstorming the subtitle. Also, my deepest thanks for sharing her computer expertise and showing me the idiosyncrasies of email and helping me to expedite this process.

I want to thank Brian Novak for his literary advice. When I thought I was nearly finished, he showed me the error of my ways.

And finally, I want to thank the staff at Author House. They displayed an innate amount of patience and understanding guiding me from beginning to end through the production process.

My life was a thrill ride from the moment I was born; through an exciting and adventurous Mid-western childhood that evolved into a distinguished thirty-year Military career; and culminated with a quiet retirement in a small picturesque New England community.

My lineage is Scotch-Irish. My ancestors settled primarily in Tennessee and North Carolina; and eventually families migrated west across the country to California. My immediate family migrated from Indiana to Nebraska and I did a turn around and started a branch in Massachusetts. I was never much of a follower.

As a young soldier, I was fortunate to have been selected to be part of the cadre of one of four newly formed specialized units assigned to the United States Army Special Forces. History has described us as extraordinary men. I consider us as fortunate to have served. The units were assigned around the world and each had a unique mission. Whether in war time or peace, when they were on the active rolls, the units served with distinction and honor and received recognition from our government by being awarded Meritorious and Presidential Unit Citations (MUC) and (PUC). I served in three of the four units. They were the Special Operations Detachments (SOD).

The 400th Special Operations Detachment (Airborne) was the first unit formed and was assigned to the 1st Special Forces Group (Airborne) on Okinawa; the 402nd Special Operations Detachment (Airborne) was assigned at Bad Toelz, Germany and later Fort Devens, Massachusetts with the 10th Special Forces Group (Airborne); the 408th Special Operations Detachment (Airborne) was assigned to the 8th Special Forces Group (Airborne) in Panama; and my first unit, the 403rd Special Operations Detachment (Airborne) was assigned to the 3rd Special Forces Group (Airborne) at Fort Bragg, North Carolina and in late 1966, under secret Department of the Army orders, we were assigned to the 5th Special Forces Group (Airborne) in the Republic of South Viet Nam. The National Security Agency (NSA) wasn't pleased with this last development because we all had Top Secret security clearances and had access to Special Compartmented Information (SCI) and NSA did not want us to actively participate in operations in a war zone. They initially attempted to restrict and control our activities. That plan didn't work.

As time went on and missions evolved and changed, so did the SODs. In the early 1970s, the 8th Special Forces Group was inactivated and along with it, the 408th SOD. As the Viet Nam War was winding down for U.S. Forces, the 5th Special Forces Group was reassigned to Fort Bragg and the 403rd SOD was inactivated. The 1st Special Forces Group on Okinawa was inactivated in early 1975, and the 400th SOD was attached to the United States Army Center for Special Warfare at Fort Bragg, North Carolina. Once the Headquarters for U.S. Army Special Forces decided what to do with us, we were again reassigned to the 5th Special Forces Group (Airborne), Fort Bragg, North Carolina.

After serving in two conventional units in Germany in the early 1980s, I was assigned to the 10th Special Forces Group at Fort Devens, Massachusetts in late 1984. My personal mission was to form and staff a new battalion. On day one, the battalion consisted of two people, the Battalion Commander and me. Our marching orders were to be completely operational within thirty days. We had carte blanche to hand-pick our staff. The Colonel selected the officers and I selected the enlisted personnel. We were up and running in record time. I implemented soldier programs for the enlisted soldiers. Although the programs were new to the 10th Group, they were really a continuation of programs I had implemented in Germany. The end result was I mentored the Group Soldier of the Year and the Group NCO of the Year just as I had mentored one soldier in Germany who became the United States Army Europe Soldier of the Year and the Association of the United States Army Europe Soldier of the Year.

The Department of the Army reassigned me to the United States Army Intelligence School one year later. I served in a myriad of positions from leading trainees to forming the United States Army Intelligence School Noncommissioned Officer Academy to serving in Directorate positions. I was also Chairman of the New England Chapter of the Noncommissioned Officer Association of the United States of America.

In 1991, I was assigned to the 470th Military Intelligence Brigade at Corozal, Panama. It was personally and professionally a very rewarding assignment. In 1993, I was given my final assignment to the United States Army Special Operations Command at Fort Bragg, North Carolina. My Military career had come full circle. I started as a Private First Class in Special Forces at Fort Bragg and my career would end as a Sergeant Major in Special Forces at Fort Bragg. This final assignment was probably the most important I had ever undertaken, especially in this time of war. For two years, I was head of the Special Operations Command Military Intelligence Relook Task Force that determined intelligence support requirements for United States Army Special Operations through the year 2020. The results of the Task Force have been quite evident during the past eight years in Iraq and Afghanistan.

On July 1st, 1995 I officially became a civilian. For six months after I retired, I received phone calls asking questions. Then one day, the phone calls stopped. I dabbled in local and state politics and did community volunteer work. I represented the City of Fitchburg, Massachusetts for four years on the Board of Directors, Montachusett Opportunity Council and I was an Associate Member on the Board of Directors for Worcester County Homeless Veterans, Inc. Off and on I worked in retail in automotive, home electronics and entertainment. The past few years I have worked in retail selling appliances at Best Buy in Marlborough, Massachusetts. I belong to a professional and social network in the organization that has grown from a few members to over 25,000 strong. We have a voice and corporate listens. As my career went full circle in the Army, I have progressed from Serving My Nation to being a member of Blue Shirt Nation.

THE TROLL

The Troll on the cover of this book was given to me by my Mother shortly before I left for Vietnam. It is approximately three inches tall. When she gave it to me, it had long white hair that formed a cone. At some point through the years, I gave it a haircut. The Troll's clothing consisted of an olive drab shirt, little trousers and shiny black shoes. The Troll also had an ammunition belt, a rifle, and a Green Beret.

The forty-two months I served in Vietnam, the Troll stayed nice and comfortable in the left breast pocket of my jungle fatigues. Whenever I went into the jungle, it was in the left breast pocket of my tiger stripes.

I had written a letter home that my Troll had lost its rifle. One of my sisters-Margie, Candy or Maxie-sent me a GI Joe rifle that was a replica of an M-16 rifle. The Troll was armed again.

As I received promotions, I would pin rank on the Troll. Although I busted him to Private when he lost his rifle. He got his rank back when I was promoted to Staff Sergeant.

When I was on flight status in 1973, the Troll stayed in the left breast pocket of my flight suit. The Troll has been in Vietnam, Cambodia, Laos, Thailand, Korea, Germany, Panama, Mexico, Peru and Honduras.

For many years, the Troll was a desk ornament. Then after I retired, it was forgotten packed away in a box for over ten years. I had mentioned the Troll online in a Blue Shirt Nation story and people asked me about it. I retrieved the Troll and it became my online persona on Blue Shirt Nation. The Troll is my avatar for Blue Shirt Nation, Facebook and Twitter. The Troll is me.

BOOK 1

Circa 1930. A caravan of dark-colored sedans followed a long driveway toward a farm house somewhere in Indiana. The cars stopped in front of the farm house and a lone figure walked up to the front porch and knocked on the door.

The farmer answered the door and the man asked permission for himself and his companions to stay in the farmer's barn overnight. Permission was granted. In the early evening, the farmer's wife delivered a meager dinner to their guests.

The following morning the lone figure once again walked up to the front porch and knocked on the door. When the farmer answered the door, he was handed one hundred dollars and that's how my Grandfather met Al Capone.

THE LITTLE GIRL AND THE COAL TENDER

The Great Depression. Indiana winter 1932-33. Each day, a little girl and her older brother would have a pile of snowballs near the railroad tracks that ran past their house. Every morning a freight train would roll by and the coal tender had a little pile of coal. He had a big, broad smile for the little children and would throw pieces of coal toward them as they threw snowballs at the train. They would wave, pick up the coal, and run into their house with it. This is how the Indiana farm family stayed warm that year.

The Great Depression. Indiana winter 1933-34. The little girl and her brother exchanged snowballs for coal with the nice coal tender for another winter.

The Great Depression. Indiana winter 1934-35. Only the little boy, Norman, was waiting at the railroad tracks for the coal tender. Trading snowballs for coal wasn't as much fun anymore, but life goes on. The little girl had contracted polio in the summer and was in a special hospital for children in Chicago. The little girl was only six years old and spent the remainder of her childhood undergoing several painful operations and muscle grafting, and medieval stretching racks so her arms and legs wouldn't become horribly deformed. When sleeping, if it was possible, her appendages were tied to bedposts so they wouldn't atrophy.

The little girl was a fighter. Growing into her teen years, she went from bed-ridden, to a wheelchair, to crutches, to using canes and finally, walking unassisted. She worked hard her whole life thereafter, became a successful businesswoman, and in the interim, raised seven children. My Mother is 81 years old today.

My Mom and Dad, when they were children, each knew President and Mrs. Roosevelt. My parents didn't know each other as young children, but each had a special place in the hearts of the President and First Lady.

For my Dad, it was a joyous occasion and he brought happiness to them. For my Mom, it was one year and four months of heartache and pain which was shared by all.

I'll start at the beginning. My Dad was born on February 8, 1925 at Rossville, Illinois. My Mom was born on August 4, 1928 at Remington, Indiana. By the age of 10, my Dad was a child radio star with the Grand Ole Opry. He was a Country Western vocalist and could make a harmonica sing. As I was growing up, my family and anyone who was in range, would listen to him play the harmonica. It was beautiful. Whenever my parents went anywhere that had music, my Dad was always asked to sing and play his harmonica. Dad was known as "Little Davey Carden" and he wore a cowboy outfit with vest and large brimmed cowboy hat that was creased at the center. He sang on Friday nights at Radio Station WDAN, Danville, Illinois. As my Mother puts it, "He sang with Little Jimmy Dickens, Minnie Pearl and that bunch." Dad introduced me to Minnie Pearl when I was eleven or twelve years old when she was part of a troupe that performed at the Civic Auditorium in downtown Fremont, Nebraska.

Over the course of several months, the White House corresponded with my grandparents. My grandfather also had some notoriety which I addressed earlier. The White House requested that my Father sing for President Roosevelt's birthday. My Father was taken to Washington, DC and he performed for the President of the United States. After my Father's funeral, my Mother and I sat on the floor in a room that contained memorabilia of their lives. I didn't know about any of this before because my Dad wanted it that way. I knew he had a great singing voice and the things he could do with a harmonica, but I never knew he was a child radio star. I asked my Mother why he didn't continue his singing career and she replied, "His voice changed."

My Mother first met the Roosevelts in 1936 when she was eight years old. She and the President each had something in common.

They had polio. My Mother contracted polio in 1934 when she was six years old. Polio was a devastating, frightening disease and people were scared. The medical field was in the Dark Ages. For two years, my Mother was tortured with experiments. The thinking at the time was to stretch her limbs so they wouldn't become deformed and to tie her feet and arms to the bed posts to prevent atrophy when she returned to her bed after therapy. In 1936 she was admitted to the Billings Hospital in Chicago which was designated as the National Research Center for Polio. President Roosevelt was also treated there and Mrs. Roosevelt would often spend time with the children. Polio was a national epidemic. My Mother spent one year and four months at Billings where she underwent many painful operations. She told her Mother that she wouldn't live to be ten and that she was going to embrace life to the fullest until her death.

The doctors at Billings had done all they could. As a footnote, Billings later became Cooke County Hospital, the place I was born. My Mother was transferred from Billings to Burnham City Hospital in Champagne, Illinois. There she underwent more operations that included bone and muscle transplants. She was told by the doctors that she would never walk again. She progressed from being bedridden to cumbersome leg-braces and a wheel chair to walking with crutches to walking canes to walking with braces to finally walking unassisted without braces. She walked across the stage for her High School graduation and she walked down the aisle for her wedding. My whole life, my Mother was strong willed and an over achiever. Now I know why.

Research for information about my parents consisted of many hours on the phone with my Mother to get factual historical data to put together bits and pieces of their lives. I understand why I was the child I was and the adult I became. I owe it all to these two wonderful people who grew up during the Great Depression and made a good life for themselves and the seven children they raised, of which, I was the eldest. My parents were the epitome of Middle America. My Dad was a cross-country semi-truck driver and my Mother was a waitress. When I was a freshman in high school, my Mother bought the restaurant that had employed her for many years. I worked for her on weekends and every Friday and Saturday night there was always a line of people waiting for one to two hours. There were other restaurants and diners in Fremont, but people wanted to eat at her place.

In an earlier story, I wrote about my paternal grandfather and Al Capone. My grandfather entered state politics and went on, in the late 1930's, to become the Sheriff of Benton County, Indiana. This had bearing on my Father's teenage years which will become evident later on.

My Mother grew up in Fowler, Indiana and my Father grew up in Boswell, Indiana. Highway 41 separated the two towns by 10 miles. They never knew each other personally as children, but my Mother used to listen to my Father on the radio as he would sing and play the harmonica. Listening to my Father's singing is one of the very few pleasant memories my Mother has as a child. Although my Father lived ten miles away and they had never met, as a young teenager, my Mother was well aware of the antics of my Father and his three older brothers, Harold, Johnny and Karl. My Father's name was David.

My Father and uncles were, in themselves, a motorcycle gang. The four of them were Fonzie, James Dean and Marlon Brando all rolled into one, before there was a Fonzie, James Dean or Marlon Brando. They didn't do anything illegal, but they were mischievous; or as my Mother puts it, "ornery." The Carden boys would ride their motorcycles or drive their Dad's police car on Saturday nights through Lafayette, Indiana because that's where all the fun was. My Father took a break from the Lafayette fun, lied about his age, and joined the Army after

Pearl Harbor. He was a bomber tailgunner, shot down over the South Pacific, did island hopping with the Infantry, was wounded and spent a year in the hospital at Oahu, Hawaii.

Sergeant David Edward Carden returned to the United States on a hospital ship. He went home to Boswell and picked up with his brothers where he had left off. That's when he met my Mother.

My Mother was a Royce, of the Rolls Royce people. However, her side of the family was so far removed that they weren't even a memory, until Rolls Royce went bankrupt. Then she was getting phone-calls from all over the world. That's another story.

My Mother was a fighter. She won the long battle over her childhood illness and she was from then on a hard worker. Today she would be called an over achiever. As a teenager, she worked in the Chocolate Shop in Fowler, Indiana. She is very proud and takes pride in her job as a "Soda Jerk." As she proudly declares, "I was a darn good one, too!" My Father and his brothers would go to Fowler, park their motorcycles outside the Chocolate Shop, and go inside. My Father made it very clear that his brothers would be on their best behavior, or as he used to tell me, he'd "take them all on, singly or one at a time." It was very wise of them to listen to their little brother. My Father used to wait for my Mother to finish work and then give her a ride home on his motorcycle. When they got married, my Mother was 17 years old and my Father was 20 years old. My Father's motorcycle riding days were over and they lived in Fowler until they moved to Fremont, Nebraska in 1952. That is when my personal adventures began.

I was born at Cooke County Hospital, Chicago, Illinois on May 16, 1947. My entrance into this world was difficult at best. I was a breech baby. As far as improvements in technology and this type of difficult birth, nothing has really changed. Nothing had ever been easy and life itself was a challenge for my Mother, so why should having a baby be any different? We both survived this time.

The morning of the seventh day of my Mother's mandatory stay in the hospital, my Father picked us up for the ride home to Fowler, Indiana. It was a joyful day for the new Carden family. My Father was driving and my Mother had me cradled in her arms in the front seat next to him. We were on a thoroughfare in the city and my Parents were enjoying their leisurely ride home. On the right! A dump truck ran a stop sign and plowed into our car hitting the passenger door dead center. My Mother lurched forward and tried to protect me with her body.

We were all transported to the nearest hospital. It was Catholic. My Father was the least injured and came out of it with a black eye. My Mother received a pummeling on the right side of her body. In addition, her face had hit the dashboard, which was solid metal. She sustained serious injuries and an oral surgeon was called in to perform corrective surgery inside her mouth. I was crushed, literally. I had internal injuries and my right leg was broken in many, many places. A Priest was summoned for me. I was baptized and read last rites. Surgeons held my leg together with pins from the hip bone to the ankle. The next eighteen months I was in a body cast from my chest down my right leg to my little foot. I don't know how many times the cast was changed or the pins were reset, but the medical team did a phenomenal job. The only thing that remains from that experience is a one-inch square scar on my right ankle.

Eighteen months in a body cast. I learned how to crawl dragging my right leg. I was fast. Because of the additional weight of the cast, I developed upper body strength when crawling. When the cast was removed for the final time, I started running. Never did learn how to walk, I was running too much. I was the primary reason my Mother was in good physical condition. It was difficult for her to keep up with me because she had one leg slightly shorter than the other due to her childhood illness. When I entered the Terrible Two's, my Mother was at her wits end. I gave her a run for the money. Then my Parents received joyous news. My Mother was with child. My Father was ecstatic. My Mother sat down in the middle of the living room floor and cried.

My Dad's New Truck

My Dad was a cross-country truck driver. He drove an 18 wheeler and was one of the best-ever truck drivers on the road. Dad first got behind the wheel of a big rig when he was 13 years old. He drove truck for 58 years. After my youngest sister was grown and left home, he took my Mother along with him on some trips. He had taught her how to drive an 18 wheeler over the course of many years and was more comfortable with her behind the wheel than with some experienced drivers. My Dad never had an accident when he was driving a truck. Now for the story....

Circa 1952. My Dad was employed by Little Audrey's. We moved from Indiana to Nebraska because the company opened a new office in Fremont. From this central location, my Dad hauled reefers (refrigerated trailers) to the East and West coasts and to Canada and Mexico. He preferred hauling refrigerated fresh foods or frozen food. He didn't like hauling tandem trailers or hauling swinging beef. Little Audrey's trucks were a sky blue color with a silver "Little Audrey's" logo written in cursive on the doors and the trailers were a shiny silver. In late 1952 my Dad became an owner-driver.

Dad was really proud of his new truck. It was a Freightliner and had a long front end where the engine was located. The front bumper was shiny chrome and the wheels were also chrome. It was a beautiful sky blue truck with the Little Audrey logo on the door and "David E. Carden-Owner" written below the logo. When Dad was home, my Mom, Dad, little three-year-old brother, Mike and I would all hand wash and wax the truck. Dad parked his truck on the street in front of our house because we didn't have a driveway.

It was 2:00 am and there was a lot of commotion in front of our house. Dad's truck was engulfed in flames and firemen were spraying it from their water tankers. The truck was destroyed. The fire was determined to be accidental and the cause was two little boys playing with matches and the older of the two was smoking a corn silk cigarette. I could never understand how the fire marshal came to that conclusion.

I spent my childhood and teen years in and near Fremont, Nebraska. My parents moved around between Fremont, Nickerson, Winslow and Arlington and back to Fremont. We were never more than half an hour from the Fremont city limits. I learned how to swim at the State Lakes. Going to Omaha was a big event. My parents originally lived in Fowler, Indiana, I was born in Chicago and we moved to Fremont when I was five years old. My first address was 154 Hickory Lane. The Hinky Dinky grocery store was being built in my neighborhood and my new found friends and I would play king on the mountain on the huge piles of dirt at the construction site. I literally watched a small town grow to 25,000 people. We sort of grew up together. Fremont eventually had two movie theaters down town and a drive-in movie at the edge of town. Winslow was a farming community where I went to a grade one through eight one-room school that was heated by a pot-belly stove in the center of the room. I attended elementary and middle schools in Fremont, Nickerson, Winslow and Arlington; and high school in Fremont.

It seems as we moved from town to town, I had the same friends. Maybe we were all Gypsies. Regardless, my friends were characters. There were the Blake twins. I don't think they had names; they were just the Blake twins. Their cousin, Jimmy, grew up to be a Nebraska State Trooper. Then, there were Tommy and Chucky Strong. They weren't twins, but there was less than a year between them and we were all in the same grade. Next were the House triplets, Marlene, Darlene and Pearl. Darlene was my girl friend all through high school. We lost touch until our 20th high school reunion in 1985. Then we lost touch again.

It was Christmas time and we were eight to ten years old. The school Christmas pageant was a huge event and it seemed the whole town attended. We all considered ourselves great thespians, but Tommy got the lead. The main program, in my mind, was our skit. This is circa 1955-56. Cowboys are the rage…The Lone Ranger, Hop-A-Long Cassidy, Lash LaRue, etc. So, the main attraction (like I said, in my mind) was our skit: "Randolph the Two-Gun Cowboy." Music was to the tune of Gene Autry's song, "Rudolph, The Red-Nosed Reindeer."

Tommy was Randolph and Chucky and I were relegated to support players in the saloon as poker players along with most of the other kids in town.

"RANDOLPH THE TWO-GUN COWBOY" Randolph the two-gun cowboy / Had two very shiny guns / And if you ever saw them / You would turn around and run / All of the other cowboys / Used to laugh and call him names / They never let poor Randolph / Join in any poker games / Then one foggy Friday night / The Sheriff came to say / Randolph with your guns so bright / Won't you guide my posse tonight? / Then how the cowboys loved him / As they shouted off with glee / Randolph the two-gun cowboy / You'll go down in history!

We all pretended to play poker and Tommy walked around the stage twirling his shiny guns. To this day, I believe Tommy got to be Randolph because he had his own shiny guns.

I know I wasn't a cool teenager, but all my friends thought it was cool that my girl friend was a triplet. They actually believed I went out with all of them.

We had a great childhood with many adventures. Things were simple then. In today's world, I can't imagine youngsters running around town, cutting through people's yards, or not being wary of grownups or strangers. Or, a group of teenagers having a spontaneous block party or just hanging out without grownups wondering what kind of mischief or trouble they would be getting into.

Guess Who's Coming to Dinner

Growing up, I don't remember my family ever eating a meal at the kitchen table. It was used by the adults to have coffee or tea; or we kids shuttled through the kitchen and sat at the table for an occasional snack.

We always had a dining room table. The table was hard wood, heavy and had at least one or two extension leaves in the center. The table had six wood chairs with padded seats and when needed, additional chairs from the set of four in the kitchen would be used. All of our primary meals-breakfast, lunch and dinner-were eaten at the dining room table.   Mom and Dad each sat at one end. If Dad was on the road, I sat in his chair. Whenever there was a new baby, and it seemed there were a lot of them, the baby would be in a high chair next to my Mom. Then it was a scramble to get as far away from the baby as possible.

It seemed that whenever Dad came home from a trip, it was always around dinner time. The reason was that he would unload his trailer at a warehouse, usually in Omaha, and then continue on to Fremont. There were guys that hung out at the warehouses waiting to unload the tractor-trailers that came in. My Dad would always hire one or two of them for a few hours work. When I was young, these men were what society called bums or winos. Dad paid them fair wages and they were appreciative for the work.

Mom always prepared more for dinner than what we really needed. She never knew what to expect. Dad would pull up in front of the house and park his truck. We knew when he got home because of the loud high-pitched "WHOOSH" sound of the air brakes. Dad would hop down from the driver's side of his truck and head for the house. Usually there would be one or two guys following him up the sidewalk. They were welcome at our house.

After dinner our guests would thank my parents for sharing food with them. I enjoyed listening to them speak as they chose their words carefully so as not to offend my Mom. Dad would then drive them back to Omaha in his car and return a couple hours later. His helpers had full stomachs and money in their pockets.

My Dad's New Car

My Dad bought his first brand new car in October 1955. It was a 1956 Ford Fairlane Coupe, dual round chrome mirrors on the front quarter panels, white body with a red leather interior and front bucket seats, state-of-the-art AM/FM radio and dual 45-degree antennas on the rear quarter panels. I think it was automatic and I have no idea what the car had for an engine. It doesn't matter.

We lived on a farm at Winslow, Nebraska and Dad would park his car in the barn during inclement weather. Every waking moment, he was polishing the car and the tons of chrome that came with it. Dad was a cross-country truck driver. Some time in the early summer of 1956 when he was driving his semi-truck taking a load West, I was riding my bicycle behind the house and got too close to the car. So close that my handle bar "keyed" the car from the rear fender across the door to the front fender. Not a good thing. I had a decision to make. Either run away to Mexico or tell my Mom. I didn't know where Mexico was, so I told my Mom. She was a miracle worker and the car was repaired before my Dad got home. I don't know if she ever told him, but he never let on to me.

1957 arrived. The summer was the worst drought that Nebraska had seen in over 20 years. The corn fields had rectangular cracks like a desert floor. There was one good rain the end of June and that was it. It was late at night on July 3rd. Dad was coming home from Omaha and when he got to Fremont, he turned onto Highway 77. Traffic was bumper to bumper and steady. He started to pass a car that speeded up, so he backed off, but his space had been filled by the car behind him. At the same time, a car pulled onto the highway and was headed toward him. There were six teenagers in the other car and they speeded up. Dad made a hard left to drive off the highway just as he came abreast of a steel railing small bridge that was over a culvert. When the car hit the bridge, he was propelled through the windshield and was airborne for about 100 feet. The car went through the railing and was a mangled heap in the culvert.

My Father landed in the only mud puddle in the middle of a corn field. He was transported by ambulance to the hospital in Fremont. Fortunately, there was a plastic surgeon from Lincoln visiting the hospital. I mention the type of surgeon he was because he could do tiny sutures. My Dad needed tiny sutures. He didn't have a face. His right eye was dangling by the optic nerve and one side of his nose had been severed. The doctor rebuilt his face. There was a gap in his right eye lid and from that moment forward, he slept with his right eye open. The face my Dad had on my 10th birthday wasn't the same one on my 11th birthday.

My Father looked at surviving the accident as a Miracle. For the remainder of his life, no matter where he was on a Sunday morning, he would go into the first House of Worship he saw. Religion or denomination didn't matter. He paid homage to a Supreme Being in a Church, Catholic or Protestant; or a Synagogue or Temple, or whatever was available. My religious training was confusing for a while. But my Mother took control.

SPORT

Circa 1957. Winslow, Nebraska. Sport was my dog. Lassie belonged to Jeff Miller (Tommy Rettig). Tommy Kirk and Kevin Corcoran owned Old Yeller. Sport belonged to me. Sport had Dalmatian markings and weighed about 50 pounds. He had the run of the farm and the barn was his dog house. Whenever I went exploring or rode my bike on the gravel country road, Sport would go with me.

My Mother had an electric wringer washing machine. She did her laundry when I was at school. When she washed clothes, they were hand-fed through the wringer to get the rinse water out of them. Then she would put the clothes in a clothes basket and go outside and hang them on the clothes line in the yard. Sport would hang out in the kitchen when Mom was doing laundry and he would sit on the porch and watch her as she hung clothes.

Sport was watching. Then he charged off the porch and ran past my Mother brushing against her leg. A few feet behind her, Sport attacked a diamondback rattlesnake. He had the snake in his mouth behind the head, was furiously shaking it, and never let go. The three to four foot snake was fighting back and it was making a snapping sound as Sport whipped it side to side. The snake went limp. He kept it in his mouth and walked into the woods behind the barn. Sport never came home.

THE FLASH FLOOD OF 1958

Circa 1958. Late summer. My parents moved to Arlington, Nebraska the previous year from Winslow. They never really moved far from Fremont. Directions to our house were easy. West on Highway 30 for five miles; north on the first country road for two miles; turn right on the first tractor path and follow it down a gradual winding slope for one fourth of a mile. At the end was a clearing similar to a cul-de-sac. On the right was a storage shed, to the front was a barn, and on the left, about 50 meters up a gradual slope, was our house.

Behind the shed was Bell Creek. It flowed into the Elkhorn River about half a mile from us. All the land on the other side of Bell Creek was corn fields that ran back to the edge of Arlington. Between the storage shed and barn was a tractor path that led up to the creek, crossed a fifty foot wooden bridge and accessed the corn fields.

My brother, Mike, and I wanted to camp out over night in our front yard. Our Mother gave us permission and we built a little camp site. We staked a tent made from blankets. We had flashlights and plenty of cookies for sustenance. We were all set. However, a blanket tent isn't much protection from mosquitoes. We didn't want to go in the house, so we went down the sidewalk to our car. One of us slept in the front seat and the other in the back.

When we awoke at daylight, there was water up to the door handles, so it had to be about two and a half to three feet deep. The water was calm where we were, but the fast moving current could easily be seen flowing behind the shed. We rolled down the front window on the house side, climbed out and waded up to the sidewalk and ran to the house.

Something had happened somewhere and the Elkhorn crested and went over its banks for a good distance on each side. Bell Creek was more like a river. I think it took a few days for the water to recede back within the banks. However, I remember playing in our driveway in about a foot of water a day or two after the flooding.

The flash flood of '58 was big news at the time. Nothing much ever really happens in Nebraska, except tornadoes. That's another story.

MY RAFT

Circa 1958. Late summer. After the flash Flood of '58, water receded back to the banks of Bell Creek. A pile of rubble had been deposited behind our shed next to the creek and my brother and I rummaged through it. We found four railroad ties to use as a base for a raft. Our intent was to ride a raft about half a mile to the Elkhorn River.

We laid out the railroad ties for a base on top of small logs. Then using wood siding from an old barn, we placed the boards on top of the ties and made a floor securing them with nails. It was simple but sturdy. We built the raft in just a few days. The raft was ready for launching.

We pushed the raft off the logs down the bank into the creek. It sank.

Sam

Circa 1959. The lazy days of summer. I was sitting on the bridge at the end of our driveway that spans Bell Creek. The bridge was the only access to the corn fields on the other side. I was dangling my legs over the side and taking aim with my .22 rifle at debris that was floating under the bridge and traveling up stream. There was an old man walking down our driveway with a fishing pole over his shoulder and he crossed the bridge behind me. He said "Hello" as he passed and started walking along the tractor path that ran parallel to the creek. The old man stopped at a bend in the creek, sat down on the bank, and cast his line into the water. Instead of twigs or tin cans floating in the water, a fishing bobber seemed to be a more lucrative target. I sat on the bridge and took aim at the bobber, which was about a hundred yards away. I fired two shots and all I did was scare the fish. The old man looked at me and I got up and went back to my house. A few moments later, my Mother answered a knock at the door. It was the old man and he said, "Good afternoon, ma'am. My name is Sam. I'm the new town marshal."

There is more to Sam's story. He was in his mid-fifties and he was a retired lawman from Texas. Sam had moved to Nebraska for a quieter life. He became a good family friend and ate Sunday dinner at our house, even after we moved back to Fremont the following year. As the years went by and I had gone away, and all my younger brothers and sisters had moved on with their lives, Sam at some point moved to Fremont. He lived in my parents' home and spent his remaining years with them. Sam died peacefully one evening watching television in their living room.

My Childhood Friend Norman

Throughout my adult life, I handled weapons and explosives and participated in activities such as parachuting, water survival, mountain climbing and rappelling, and martial arts. Safety was paramount and I owe my strict adherence to safety procedures to my childhood friend Norman.

When we were twelve or thirteen years old, the rage at school was shooting spit balls with a rubber band across study hall. I never did it I think primarily because I didn't like the taste of wadded up paper. Norman was bored with spit balls and started shooting staples. He could shoot them further and he thought it was funny. One day in study hall, Norman was shooting staples and the rubber band broke. He lost an eye. That one incident made an enormous impression on me. Because of Norman, I never participated in any form of grab-ass; nor as an adult, did I ever allow any form of grab-ass in the work place.

A few years later, Norman was hunting with his Dad on their farm. He had leaned his shotgun against a barbed wire fence. The tension of him climbing through the strands knocked the shotgun to the ground and it discharged. The pellets hit Norman on the left arm at his elbow. Doctors were able to save his arm, but for the rest of the time I knew him, his arm was always in a sling. This was 1960-61, and technology at the time didn't allow for joint replacement.

Periodically, I think of Norman and hope he went on to do great things with his life.

I grew up in Tornado Alley as millions of people have. In my lifetime, I have been inside two structures that were hit by tornadoes. The first time, it was 1952 and I was five years old and my younger brother, Mike, was three. Our Father was a cross-country semi-truck driver and he was on the road. So it was my Mother, brother and me at home in a little town in Indiana. The house we lived in didn't have a basement. Although she had grown up in Indiana, my Mother had never been exposed to the devastation of a tornado. The noise was horrendous and my young Mother took us to her bedroom, put us in my little brother's baby bed, yanked the mattress off my parents' bed, got under it and pulled the mattress down over all of us. Although we were all huddled together, we couldn't hear each other because of the deafening freight train noise. The roof of the house was blown off and a huge tree came crashing down on top of us. I believe the tree was instrumental in preventing serious injury and saving all of our lives. My Mother told me a few years ago that going into her bedroom and using her bed mattress for our protection was the only thing she could think of to do.

It was shortly after that when my parents migrated to Fremont, Nebraska. Fremont is in a valley and during tornado season, we could see the beginnings of tornadoes forming over the city and then we would hear on the news about the tornadoes that would go into the countryside. As I was growing up in Fremont and the surrounding communities, there always seemed to be a tornado somewhere in the area and my parents would drive into the country to see what had happened.

After the flash flood of '58, my parents moved from Arlington back to Fremont. Instead of renting a house, this time they bought what was at the time a huge mobile home that was 58 feet long by 10 feet wide. We lived on the edge of town at a mobile home park just a few blocks from my first home in Fremont. Life was good.

On a beautiful Saturday morning some time in the summer of 1962, my Mother and I were sitting at the kitchen table. She was drinking a cup of tea and I was drinking a Pepsi. What happened next was very quick, no slow motion stuff, just fast. Our car, which was normally parked in front of our home, went past the window. However, it wasn't our car that was in motion, it was us. A tornado had set down on the edge of town and the wind had blown us around. The front and rear of our mobile home took out the homes on each side of us.

After that, my parents bought a house with a basement in the center of town across the street from the park that had the Civil Defense emergency siren that was tested at noon on the first Saturday of every month.

When I came home from Viet Nam in early February 1970, it took me a while to adapt to the new time zone. So, I would be awake at night and sleep during the day until I adjusted. I was sleeping soundly in the downstairs guest room when that damn siren across the street went off at noon. My Mother was entertaining some of her friends in the living room when I came running through yelling "INCOMING!"

CIVICS AND ME

Circa 1960 to 1965. Shortly after my thirteenth birthday, I answered a job notice for a part-time position at the Fremont, Nebraska Chamber of Commerce. Since the job paid seventy-five cents an hour, I think I was the only person in the whole town who applied. The new office boy was ready to go to work for a couple of hours a day. Primary duties were "go-fer this, go-fer that."

Two people worked in the office, the President of the CofC and also the Mayor of Fremont, Dwight Collins; and his assistant, Mrs. VonDerlage (pronounced Von Der Log E). I think introductions were addressed as such: Dwight Collins said, "You can call me Dwight," and Mrs. VonDerlage said, "You can call me Mrs. VonDerlage." During the five years that I worked at the Chamber of Commerce, I never did learn her first name. Her name placard even said "Mrs. VonDerlage."

In addition to go-fer duties, I also folded business letters, stuffed envelopes, processed business correspondence through the postage machine; and set up and operated the lithograph machine.

What I considered my most important duty to be was to display American Flags along Main Street during federal holidays. I was paid a total of five dollars for putting up and taking down the flags. The job took three hours each time…3:00 am to 6:00 am for putting them up and 6:00 pm to 9:00 pm for taking them down. The flags were stored in a large cardboard box mounted on a push truck and I had a long wooden ladder to climb light poles to put the flags in their holders. In five years, I only fell once. I was nearly finished putting up flags when the ladder shifted toward the sidewalk side and gravity did the rest. I only fell about ten feet. The ladder hit the movie theater marquee and it exploded. I was showered with shards of glass from the neon lights. There must have been some type of alarm on the building, because the police showed up about two minutes later. That's how I got a new cart and a new aluminum ladder. Today I see men in cherry pickers displaying flags. It's not nearly as much fun as climbing up and down a ladder and hand emplacing each flag.

A NIGHT AT THE MOVIES

Circa 1960. Drive-in movie night. Little did we know, this particular drive-in movie night would be one we would never forget. Going to the drive-in movie was a special treat for the Carden kids. It meant that for an unspecified period of time, known only to our parents, we had accomplished every parent's dream…not driving them crazy. There wasn't a whole lot for a family to do in Fremont, other than going out for ice cream, and a night at the drive-in movie was much better than ice cream.

It seemed like an all day event getting ready to go to the drive-in. To save money, my Mom popped popcorn and put it in grocery bags. She would also make a batch of lemonade to take along. In case anyone is wondering, we didn't have candy because of the expense. Even today it's more expensive to buy treats at the theater than the actual ticket, some things never change. It's more than likely that my Dad may have slipped a couple beers under the driver seat of our Plymouth Valiant station wagon. He preferred a brewski over lemonade. At the time, I was the oldest of the five Carden kids; myself, Mike, Margie, Joe and Tom. Our job was to take along a pillow and blanket from each of our beds and put them in the car. At 7:00 pm we departed our home enroute to the Fremont Drive-in Theater on Route 30 at the edge of town. At 7:30 pm, my Dad had the car parked dead center, usually first or second row. During the next hour, we played on the playground under the screen along with all the other kids at the movie. The playground had a swing set, a big merry-go-round, a jungle gym, a slide and a couple of teeter-totters. It was a lot of fun running around and playing on the playground while we waited for the show to start. It may have also been good alone time for our parents in the car. Then it was about thirty minutes of refreshment stand advertising, previews, a cartoon and the giant three-minute main feature count-down clock.

Tonight's feature was an Alfred Hitchcock movie, "Psycho." My siblings and I were laying or sitting in our respective spots in the station wagon munching on popcorn and drinking lemonade. When the movie started I remember thinking that this was going to be a boring Mom and Dad movie.

And then the camera panned to a shower curtain, the background music got weird, there was a silhouette of somebody with a knife, and instantly I changed my opinion that this might be a good movie after all…that's when my Mother went into labor. And that is how my new baby sister, Candy, came into this world.

My Siblings

I was the oldest of seven children. My siblings, from older to younger were: Mike, Margie, Joe, Tom, Candy and Maxie. One of my favorite jokes is: Every family has that one weird relative. If you're sitting at the kitchen table and looking at all your relatives and don't see the weird one...guess who it is. This joke has nothing to do with my story. I just like the joke.

But, every family has a thinker. In my family, the thinker was me. I wondered about stuff...the meaning of life, why is the sky blue? Stuff like that. I wasn't very athletic. I like baseball, but couldn't throw, catch, hit or run. So I watched. In high school, I was the Vice President of FBLA (Future Business Leaders of America), a school club for thinkers.

My siblings were the athletes. I'll start with Joe. He was the middle child. Joe was an athlete in baseball and football. He was also very talented; and an accomplished musician and artist. Mike was a varsity wrestler. Tom played baseball and football. He attended college on a baseball scholarship and was drafted by Cincinnati. My sisters... Margie, Candy and Maxie all played girls' softball. Candy and Maxie played on the girls' high school softball team and they were also on the swim team.

Like I said before, I was the thinker.

MY FIRST CAR

I started driving when I was 12 or 13 years old. The vehicle was a '52 or '53 Chevy coupe with a blown transmission. However, it had reverse gear. So I drove it backwards all over a pasture. My friends didn't mind that we were only going in backward circles.

On my 16th birthday, I passed my driver's test and received a Nebraska driver's license. My first official forward-moving car was a birthday present from my parents. They gave me a 1957 Ford Fairlane coupe with a three-speed on-the-column manual transmission and a three-quarter racing cam (whatever that means). The car was black with a white knight chess piece painted on each rear quarter panel. Scripted over the knight, written in cursive, was the name "Paladin." It was a reference to the Richard Boone character on the TV show "Have Gun, Will Travel." The car had been a stock car and the owner stopped racing it. The previous owner was a character himself. He was always dressed in black and wore a black Stetson hat and silver-trimmed black leather vest. I remember him as being a little dorky. But without him I wouldn't have had a car, so I guess he was an all right guy.

I tried drag racing "Paladin" a couple of times, but the gear ratio was so low that by the time I got off the line, the race was over. Or I was just a crappy racer. We used to race on the old abandoned Highway 36 outside of town. None of the chicken stuff like racing toward a rock quarry…we didn't have one.

BOOK 2

My First Encounter with an Officer
Jump School
My First Week in Viet Nam
Martha Ray & Me
My Friend CJ Johnson
Tet '68
First Three Rows Reserved
My Brother Mike
Christmas Eve 1968
VC Charlie
Mascots
My Job in Vietnam
Charlie from Ohio
Capturing
Law and Order
The CCC Guys
Nicknames
Ranger Joe
My Mentors
My Best Friend Bob
The Soldier's Medal
Agent Orange
Mortality
Bud & Arlis
Cars
How I Met Miss Elkhart
Ski Training
Gracemary
Dominic James Ingemi
The Abilene Paradox
The Boxer and the Black Belt
Purgatory
The Super Jock
Okinawa Returned to Japan

The Fort Bragg 400th
Escape and Evasion (E&E)
Kathy & Katie
My Buddy Joe
Raymond and the Lady
Special Terrain Parachuting Techniques
Used To Be
The Carter Years
Parachute Landing Fall
Why I was in Iran
The Cute Little Lamb
Convoy Commander
Russians in Cuba
REDTRAIN
The DC Motorcycle Cop
The Marine
Why I was in Pakistan
Islamabad at Dawn
331st Army Security Agency Company
The Bully
Corrective Training
330th Electronic Warfare Aviation Company
GUARDRAIL Wine
Carl Laksmannen
My First Battalion
The School Brigade
The Buono Plan
The One-Handed Snow Shovel
The Coors Northeastern
The Intelligence School
The MP
NCOA
The Stranded Trucker
Desert Shield & Desert Storm
The Night Before Desert Storm
My Job in Panama
Captains

Jump Stories
My Swan Song
Awards, Decorations and Accoutrements
Assignments
My Retirement Ceremony

After completing Basic Combat Training at Fort Leonard Wood, Missouri, this simple country boy from Nebraska went home for a week. I then had my first experience on an airplane traveling from Omaha, Nebraska to Boston, Massachusetts. My plane landed at Logan Airport in Boston. After picking up my duffel bag from the baggage area, I had to find directions and a means of transportation to Fort Devens. I was going to school at Fort Devens but had no idea where it was located. I saw an Army captain and asked him for assistance. He told me to wait and he would be right back. When he returned, he was with two Navy Shore Police. He told me to go with them. I rode in the back of their police car to the South Shore and spent the night in the brig. Then the next morning, I was driven to the Massachusetts State Police Barracks at Concord, Massachusetts and turned over to them. This was a Saturday morning. The State Police transported me to Fort Devens and I was placed in custody of the Military Police. The MPs called the Regimental Staff Duty Officer at the Intelligence School and he signed for me. I was then processed at the Regiment, assigned to a company in the Training Battalion, restricted to my barracks for the weekend, and instructed to report to my First Sergeant first thing Monday morning. I knew my Army career was finished. The First Sergeant asked me what happened and I told him that I had never travelled before and I had asked an Army captain for help getting to Fort Devens and the next thing I knew I was arrested by two Navy guys, spent the night in jail, was turned over to state troopers who turned me over to MPs who turned me over to another Army captain who restricted me to the barracks for the weekend and told me to report to my First Sergeant first thing Monday morning. I have stated chronologically and factually what happened, but in reality I was probably an 18 year-old scared babbling idiot. The First Sergeant looked me straight in the face and said, "Don't worry about it."

At that moment, I think I realized I wanted to be a First Sergeant. For me, it happened 15 years later. And one of my first acts as a First Sergeant was to tell a young soldier not to worry about being arrested the night before. He had been drinking at a party, so his pregnant wife was driving home which was corroborated by people at the party. She went into labor and hit a guardrail, which caused extensive damage to the side of their car. He put her in the back seat and drove to the hospital emergency room. Staff assisted with his wife, a policeman had seen him driving in and afterwards told him to move his car. But before doing so, the policeman smelled alcohol on his breath and he was arrested. He told the policeman what happened, but after looking at the damage to the car, the policeman didn't believe him. I had a chance to check things out before he saw me and was able to have it handled administratively instead of judicially.

The encounter of this young Private with the Army captain at Logan Airport was a significant emotional event. Throughout my career, I was on the side of the underdog and had a distrust of young officers, although older officers seemed to be all right. As a young Noncommissioned Officer, there were a few run-ins that could have been career ending. But level heads prevailed and I was proven to be right. I did not allow anyone, regardless of rank, to impugn the integrity or trample on the dignity of any soldier.

It was November 1965 and I was attending Military Intelligence training at Fort Devens, Massachusetts. A Special Forces recruiting team was looking for volunteers for a new elite unit. They said that they couldn't tell us anything about the unit other than it was tough, physical training and their members went on dangerous, classified missions. I was more intrigued by what they didn't say than what was said in their formal presentation.

I, along with approximately 60 other soldiers from Fort Devens volunteered and went through one day of physical torment. This included but was in no way limited to dropping down to do push-ups with a foot planted squarely in your back adding torque to your push-ups or just being placed in a front-leaning-rest position for an indeterminate period of time. There was harassment, which was more akin to a drill sergeant screaming at your face at the top of his lungs phrases such as, "did your momma have any kids that lived," and the unforgettable, "my sister has bigger balls than you." Somehow this was supposed to be a form of motivation to work harder; personally these so called "pep talks" and forms of intimidation never motivated me. If those things weren't enough, then came the running over every inch of the ten square miles of the main post of Fort Devens. These drills ran from early morning before sun-up until after sun-down. At 18½ years old, although tiring, it was fun and an accomplishment. Throughout the day, people quit because they couldn't handle the intense personal stress. By the time the recruitment screening was over, there were only two of us left.

The recruiters were all base cadre of a new Special Forces unit at Fort Bragg, North Carolina. Some of them had become my good friends through the following years and some of them didn't. I was a young Nebraska country boy and quite impressionable. Each recruiter wore a "blue rifle" badge on his uniform and I wanted to wear one on mine. A year later, while under fire in Viet Nam, it dawned on me that the "blue rifle" was a Combat Infantryman Badge (CIB) and it was earned by being shot at by a hostile force. And, it seemed, I was continuously earning that badge. The CIB is a badge of honor for the infantryman as the Combat Action Badge (CAB) today is an honor for soldiers in other branches of the Army and the Combat Action Ribbon is worn with honor by United States Marines.

I had previously submitted a request for Officer Candidate School (OCS) and the paperwork for Special Forces was hand-carried to Department of the Army by the recruiting team. The Special Forces request was approved. I don't know what happened to the OCS request.

I was an Honor Graduate in January 1966 and thusly promoted to Private First Class. Having received my new promotion I went home to Nebraska for two weeks leave prior to my reporting to jump school. Then it was on to Fort Benning, Georgia "HOME OF THE AIRBORNE." Only in the Army for nine months and I was already a Private First Class. I was really excited about the adventure before me. However, my Basic Airborne Course (BAC) class was placed on hold and I performed KP (Kitchen Police) for 30 days (really suck duty in the Army). Then I had a start date, and mysteriously, the original class that had my new start date was placed on KP. Kitchen Police was a good management tool at Fort Benning. At least the pots and pans and grease traps were always clean. Prior to starting class, I was issued new boots because mine were ruined from working in the grease trap.

March 1966: My class starts. THREE WEEKS (1) Ground Week (2) Tower Week (3) Jump Week and Graduation. Nowhere in those three weeks was there scheduled a whole lot of time for sleep. My class had people from all the Services. The Marines had to prove they were better than the Army so they would run in circles around our formations as we were running forward. I would venture to guess their circular running was three times as far as our running and they arrived at the same location as we did at the same time. Basic Airborne Course students were divided into groupings of fifteen people. These groupings were named sticks. My stick leader, and the person who was ultimately responsible for me and my whereabouts, was an Air Force Captain. All students were treated the same, regardless of rank...Like dirt.

Then, there was this 40-ish sleazy, skinny, bald headed bakery truck driver tattle-tale buck sergeant in my stick from a Fort Benning unit that for some reason which I'll never know took it upon himself to tell the Air Force Captain every minor indiscretion or little thing I did wrong for which the Air Force Captain was compelled and bound to act upon. This usually meant pushups for me. And believe me, I did a lot of pushups…pushups directed by the instructors because one of them had learned my name…and pushups directed by the Air Force Captain because of the sleaze ball bakery truck driver. If nothing else, I think I gained a couple of inches around my biceps.

Week one was mostly physical…which mainly consisted of formation running and pushups (of which I must have done thousands) and practicing Parachute Landing Falls (PLF) from four-foot platforms while suspended from a Swing Landing Trainer. About half my class made it through week one. Each night after dinner, we would collapse on our bunks completely exhausted. Arm and leg muscles ached at the end of the first couple of days, but were feeling better and better toward the end of the week because we were being physically conditioned.

Week two was fun. More running and pushups, but we also got to practice jumping out of 34-foot towers in dummy parachute harnesses. Thirty four feet is the point at which you lose depth perception; 34 or 304, it looks the same. So you climb up spiraling stairs inside the wobbly 34-foot tower, stand in the door, and jump out in a tight body position counting ONE THOUSAND, TWO THOUSAND, THREE THOUSAND, FOUR THOUSAND, grab your risers, check your imaginary canopy for holes, slide down a long cable, spread eagle so the guys at the end of the slide can catch you when you pass them and bounce off the end of the cable back toward them. Then, you run back to the tower and do it again.

The Wind Machine: A giant fan that blows a mini-hurricane. You're in your harness, lying on your back, hooked up to a canopy, the fan blows, and you're off. You have to engage the quick release on your canopy to prevent serious injury from being dragged. This exercise is repeated about a dozen times a day until it becomes a natural act of disengaging the parachute canopy.

I shall interject here that we ate three meals a day; at least one hot meal at the mess hall or from a mess hall on wheels. Breakfast for the most part was "shit-on-a-shingle" (either chipped beef or ground beef and gravy over toast), bacon or sausage, pancakes, toast, milk or chocolate milk, and coffee; any combination or all, provided you could eat it all in the three minutes allocated for meals once you sat down.

To gain access to the mess hall, we marched across a wooden

bridge that spanned a four-foot wide ditch. Then we had to traverse the horizontal ladder (monkey bars) that was located just before the entrance to the mess hall. We were told never to jump over the ditch because ONLY AIRBORNE SOLDIERS COULD JUMP OVER THE DITCH. I mention this because, 12 years later, when I was a Senior Noncommissioned Officer on Temporary Duty at Fort Benning, I looked for and found that stupid little ditch and successfully jumped over it in my dress green uniform…spit-shined paratrooper boots and all.

Week two. The final day. The 250-foot Tower. This was a make or break. Your harness risers are hooked to a real parachute canopy and you are hoisted 250 feet into the air and dropped. All of your training up to this point depends on whether you survive this one event. If you paid attention, learned well and did what you were supposed to do, you performed a good Parachute Landing Fall when you hit the ground, engaged your quick release, jumped up and moved out smartly. If not, you had a free trip to the hospital and a plane ticket home. Being hoisted 250 feet into the air was an exhilarating experience. It was a relatively slow trip to the top and I relished the time looking out over the Fort Benning landscape. There was a noticeable jolt as the canopy was released. The descent was faster than going up and the wind blew me away from the tower which was, in my estimation, a good thing. As I approached the ground, there was an instructor with a bull horn telling me to not look at the ground but at the horizon and to prepare for a landing. After landing, the instructor recorded my student number for successfully completing that portion of the training.

Week three was Jump Week which consisted of five parachute jumps from an altitude of 1,250 feet. Three daytime, one nighttime, and one in full combat equipment. The first daytime jump was out the tailgate of a C-119 cargo plane. It had two booms that extended at 30 degrees beyond the back of the aircraft and a third horizontal boom that connected the ends. Our instructors told us to jump up and out and try to tap the overhead boom which was physically impossible. This may have been a ploy to keep people from looking down, way down, at the ground. It was very noisy inside the aircraft due to the sound of the propeller-driven engines. Communication was primarily accomplished through a hand tap on your shoulder or watching hand gestures that had been imbedded into your brain that corresponded with vocal instructions for preparation to go through the tail gate or the door and jump from the airplane. There wasn't time to be afraid because our training had prepared us for what we were about to do.

Stand up, hook up, and shuffle to door. For my first jump, I was somewhere in the middle of the stick and being prodded along like cattle in a chute being prodded toward the slaughter house. Then the person in front of me disappeared and I was looking straight ahead at open sky. Next it was a vigorous jump up and out while maintaining a tight body position. My parachute streamed out of the back pack and I felt a hard jerk as my canopy opened and caught the air. A quick check for holes or tears in the canopy, and then it was a slow ride down to the ground; all the while looking around to ensure that that there weren't any other jumpers in my immediate vicinity. Upper body strength was very important, thus the reason for all the pushups. The T-10 wasn't easily steerable. In order to turn, you had to reach up as high as you could, grasp a front riser with one hand and the opposite rear riser with the other hand, and then simultaneously pull both risers down into your chest. Thusly, you could turn right or left depending on which risers you grasped. When turning, you also speeded up your descent because you were spilling air from the canopy. If you wanted to descend faster, all you had to do was pull both front risers down into your chest and you would drop like a rock. I just went along for the ride.

Parachute Landing Fall. There's an old joke that says it's not the fall that kills you, but the sudden stop at the end. At approximately 100 feet above the ground, it's time to prepare to land. A good PLF (Parachute Landing Fall) is tantamount to a good parachuting life experience. Arms extended, elbows locked, hands grasping front risers firmly; eyes straight ahead and on the horizon; feet and knees together, knees slightly bent, toes pointed downward; and await the inevitable. Simultaneously, in a split second, several things occur: Your feet touch the ground, your risers are pulled down into your chest while bringing your clenched hands and forearms together in front of your face as a source of protection, your knees are shifted right or left depending on your forward momentum, and as your knees are shifted and your body twists, your buttock next touches the ground followed by the push-up muscle behind your shoulder. You've landed successfully. So, get up, gather up your parachute and walk to the turn in point.

Jumps one, two and three went great. The night jump was the scary one. Once you focus your eyes, you can ascertain your rate of descent and distinguish ground features. When you prepare to land, keep your eyes on the horizon. As the horizon gets lower, so do you. Execute a good Parachute Landing Fall, recover your equipment and turn it in. The combat equipment jump was also the graduation jump.

The graduation jump was at a Drop Zone that had bleachers for spectators and a grandstand for distinguished guests and speakers. Moms and Dads and Friends and Relatives were there. The plane flew horizontally at 1,250 feet in front of the bleachers and grandstand. The graduating class jumped out the door.

After landing and turning in equipment, there was a formation in front of the bleachers and grandstand. Dignitaries talked about how great we are and how we're going off to do miraculous and wondrous things. The Basic Parachutist Badge was pinned on each of our chests. WE ARE UNITED STATES ARMY PARATROOPERS and it's time to get the hell out of Dodge before somebody changes their mind and says we have to do something else. The Marines hung a sheet with a caricature of the USMC Bulldog on the Fort Benning water tower. And the sleazy buck sergeant bakery truck driver? I don't know whatever happened to him and I really don't care.

Every challenge I have had in my life, I have approached in the same manner. I don't know why, it's just something I did. That is: No matter what I am required to do, I tell myself that thousands of people before me have done it and there is no reason on earth why I can't do it too. Only in the twilight years of my life have I reflected that although I followed that principle, there were thousands or tens of thousands of people before me that didn't make it. Never once have I ever hesitated. On March 26th, 1966 I reported to Fort Bragg, North Carolina. The other kid never showed up.

My First Week in Viet Nam

Circa 1966. Late fall. We debarked from the U.S.S. General George Weigel at Cam Rahn Bay, Republic of South Viet Nam. There was a convoy of trucks waiting for us. We loaded our equipment and personal belongings and climbed into the backs of the trucks. We each had an M-14 Rifle and were informed there was no ammunition in country for our weapons. So we held on to dead weight for the unarmed trip to the Headquarters, 5th Special Forces Group (Airborne) at Nha Trang. I don't remember how long the trip was, but I distinctly remember how beautiful the countryside was looking at it from the back of the truck I was riding in. The trip was uneventful.

We spent the next few days at Nha Trang being in processed and getting our assignments throughout the country. I was assigned to the camp designated B-24 at Kontum in the Central Highlands. We were issued jungle fatigues, tiger stripes (the camouflage uniform Special Forces wore on combat operations), and weapons. My primary weapon was a World War II and Korean War vintage .30-caliber M-2 Automatic Rifle and a .45-caliber pistol as a side arm. I also had a snub nose .38-caliber revolver as a personal weapon. While I was still at Nha Trang, an old pro took me under his wing. He took my Carbine and gave it back later with modifications. The shoulder stock and barrel had been sawed off and suspension line and a snap link had been added to secure the weapon to my person. The modifications were to prevent the weapon from being tangled in underbrush in the jungle. At a later time, I was quite grateful.

Those of us going to the Central Highlands flew in a C-119 cargo transport to a small airfield outside Kontum. We were then driven to the camp. After getting acquainted with our surroundings, we received our first culture shock. A group of Montangards carried a tiger into camp slung under a long bamboo pole. They had killed it a couple of kilometers outside our camp. After seeing the tiger, a good friend of mine said that was it, tigers were not in his contract and nothing would get him to go into the jungle. He was going to stay inside the camp for his whole tour. Of course he as well as I was at the bottom of the totem pole, and we were outside the wire in no time following and learning. One thing I learned was that tigers were known to drag people from foxholes in the middle of the night. Also, there were nasty creatures in the jungle. They included spiders, scorpions, fire ants and snakes; the bamboo krait being the deadliest. It had a nick name as the bamboo two-step. I never met one personally and had no intention of ever meeting one.

I was a 19 year-old kid in December 1966 when I first met Martha Ray. She came to my Special Forces camp at Kontum, Viet Nam as part of a USO tour. It was just her and her entourage. Martha Ray was a movie star and a Lieutenant Colonel in the Army Nurse Corps. This trip was a little entertaining and performing her Military duty. She was good people.

It was early evening and I had just returned to camp after being out for about 10 days. We had a small one-room shack that served as a club and I headed over to get a Coke (I am a non-drinker. Picked up smoking, but never acquired a taste for alcohol). I was unshaven, dirty and probably smelled a little ripe. Maggie was sitting in the corner of the room at the poker table and a group of guys was standing around watching the game. I walked over and some of my friends were playing and there was an open seat. She looked at me and said, "Have a seat, young Sergeant." I told her I didn't have any money with me and a voice behind me said, "Here, kid." Sergeant Major Johnson, the Camp Sergeant Major, handed me $200 in MPC's (Military Payment Certificates…script used in Viet Nam that served as U.S. dollars). So I sat down.

Here I was, a country boy from Nebraska playing poker with a movie star. Golly! The game was Five Card Stud. One hole card and four up. Best hand wins. Hole cards were dealt around the table and one card up. My hole card was an Ace. Maggie had a deuce showing. Bets all around. Next card paired my top card and Maggie's deuce. More bets, some people folded. Third card up I had an Ace and Maggie had a face card. This round of betting just left her and me. The last card up didn't do either of us any good. The last of the $200 went into the pot and I was calculating my winnings. Aces over had her two pair beat. I gingerly turned over my Ace and she said, "Nice hand, young Sergeant, but not good enough," as she turned over her third deuce. That's how I met Martha Ray.

My Friend CJ Johnson

Circa 1967. Early fall. Replacements were rolling into Kontum because the initial group from Fort Bragg was approaching DEROS (Date Estimated Rotation Over Seas). In other words, they were going home. CJ Johnson was a part of the replacement group. CJ was a mountain of a young man and towered over anyone near him. Although time may have exaggerated his size in my mind, I believe he had to turn sideways to go through a doorway. CJ was also one of the nicest guys in the world.

Our living quarters inside the compound consisted of a Military canvas medium size tent commonly referred to as a GP Medium Tent (General Purpose Medium Tent). We each had our own living space with a Military cot that was enclosed by a mosquito net. The sides of the tent were rolled up during the daytime to keep the heat out and rolled down at night to keep the insects, reptiles and rodents out.

CJ's cot was positioned directly across from mine. The foot of his cot was opposite the foot of my cot with a walkway between. The rest of the occupants were aligned the same way. After CJ's welcoming party, all NUGS (new guys) had a welcome party, we retired for the evening. Just before sunrise, CJ sounded like a banshee. I awoke and sat upright with a .45 and flashlight, as did several others in the tent. CJ was sitting upright in his mosquito net enclosed cot holding a huge black rat by the neck. He ripped open his mosquito net and threw the rat through the tent doorway. The rat had climbed into CJ's cot and bit his foot.

During the next week or so, CJ went through a series of rabies shots in his stomach. Each morning at 11:00 am, CJ would walk across the compound to the dispensary to get his shot. It seems that as the days wore on, his walking was slower and his trek to the dispensary took longer. Then, the final day arrived and CJ got his last shot.

CJ was sleeping soundly in his mosquito net enclosed cot when the unthinkable happened again. He was not a happy camper. And he was very adamant about not taking the rabies series again. As it turns out, whatever the rabies treatment was in 1967, it could only be administered to an individual only once in a lifetime. He couldn't have been treated again. CJ's nickname was RATMAN.

Tet '68

The Tet Offensive was officially begun by the Viet Cong and North Vietnamese Army during the early morning hours of January 30th, 1968 and was conducted through September 23rd, 1968. The official U.S. position is that the Tet Offensive terminated in June 1968 which places it within the structure of American military and political decisions to begin initial planning for withdrawal of U.S. Forces from the Republic of South Viet Nam. History and politics aside, Tet is the Vietnamese New Year and the most sacred of their holidays. Since the French were driven out in 1954 and the North and South were at war, both sides always honored a truce during the Tet holiday period. Until 1968. The North Vietnamese and Viet Cong swarmed into 25 major cities from the DMZ (Demilitarized Zone) and Hue in the north to Saigon and Can Tho in the Delta.

To get to the big city of Pleiku in the Central Highlands, they decided to trample on a little nondescript hamlet named Kontum. U.S. Military presence was my little Special Forces camp and some MACV Advisors adjacent to us. MACV (pronounced as Mack Vee) is the acronym for Military Assistance Command Viet Nam. On the opposite side of Kontum was the 24th STZ, which was a Vietnamese artillery headquarters with some American Advisors.

My camp had 16 Americans, four MACV Advisors and about 100 Montangards. Montangards are the bravest and fiercest fighters in the world. They have been suppressed by and at war with the Vietnamese since the Vietnamese became a people. They were and still are extremely loyal to Americans. The North Vietnamese and Viet Cong had a full Regiment, about 300 battle hardened soldiers. My defensive position was the .50 caliber machine gun on the north wall. With me were four "Yards." One was my ammo bearer, and the other three fired their weapons through the firing ports. Also, they each had 10 firing mechanisms for Claymore mines set up outside the four strands of concertina wire in front of the bunker. My little bunker was a fortress in itself. I also had a 57mm recoilless rifle at my disposal. The highlight of my Military career to that point was firing my recce at the steeple on top of the French mission outside the wire. My friend Paul was in charge of burning the 403rd Special Operations Detachment bunker so it wouldn't be captured. The bunker contained a multitude of classified order of battle information, classified communications equipment and codes, and a refrigerator for sandwiches, soda and beer. Losing that refrigerator caused a certain amount of grief. Paul told me several years later that the highlight of his career was burning that bunker.

The Special Forces and MACV camps were surrounded and eventually MACV was breached and personnel from that camp withdrew into the Special Forces camp. Additionally, the North Vietnamese were reinforced with another Regiment. After everything was all over, a reconnaissance team found four 122mm rockets set up in a series and aimed at the MACV compound. The rockets had misfired. There were two North Vietnamese Regiments that didn't make it to Pleiku. Tet '68 at Kontum was over, but the incursion for the Tet Offensive continued four more days throughout the country.

Circa 1968. After TET 1968, we had cleaning up to do at Kontum after the North Vietnamese and Viet Cong Chinese New Year party. Structures within our compound had to be rebuilt and reinforced; and the 403rd Operations Bunker was rebuilt using cinder blocks and sand bags all around the building for protection. I even went over to the French mission and helped repair damage from my .57mm Recoilless Rifle.

I didn't get to stay around long. In July 1968, I was reassigned to the Special Forces Operations Base "C" Team at Can Tho in the Mekong Delta. When I arrived, my first impression of the C-Team headquarters was the entrance. There was a patio outside with rows of benches set up centered on a movie screen mounted on the side of the building. Next to the screen, about one-fourth its size was a sign that read, "First three rows reserved for amputees." I wondered what I had gotten into.

Enemy forces in the Delta were primarily Viet Cong with maybe a few North Vietnamese advisors. My job was to locate them through Morse communications intercept and radio direction finding with assistance from Army and Air Force aerial radio direction finding (ARDF) specially-equipped helicopters and fixed-wing aircraft. We were able to identify and keep tabs on Viet Cong and North Vietnamese units operating in the Mekong Delta. With Can Tho as a base, I went out to different A-Teams in the Delta to assist in locating Viet Cong small units. I was fortunate to spend time with SEAL TEAM 2 at My Phuoc Tay and got to zip around in swamp boats.

After nearly a year in the Delta, I went back to the Central Highlands. I was assigned for a short while to the Special Forces Team at Ban Don, which was subordinate to Team B-23 at Ban Me Thuot. Ban Don was located on the Buon e Soup River and was also the elephant capital of Southeast Asia. Elephants were used the same as they were in Thailand. We used elephants to transport heavy equipment through the jungle and a little tidbit I learned was that elephants are deathly afraid of monkeys.

Another thing about Ban Don was the colonies of fire ants in the jungle. Fire ants were red in color and about one-eighth inch in length.

There were some fire ant colonies in mounds that were three to five feet high. In addition, they also lived in the trees and would sometimes fall on you as you were moving through the jungle. I once had the misfortune of being near a fire ant hill that had been sprayed by AK47 fire. The burning sensation of a fire ant bite is like being pricked with a hot needle. I have numerous tiny white scars on the left side of my face, my neck and forearms from being bitten by those aggressive tiny creatures.

There weren't any major enemy forces in the Ban Don area of operations, so I was sent back to Kontum after about a month of searching for North Vietnamese regimental-size infantry units.

MY BROTHER MIKE

My brother Mike is two years younger than me. Growing up, we were best friends and one or the other of us would be the instigator of some type of mischief. Our Dad's new truck when we were little is a prime example of what could happen when the two of us were together.

Mike was an athlete and a varsity wrestler in high school. He joined the Army and volunteered for Special Forces. His first assignment, same as mine, was with the 3rd Special Forces Group, Fort Bragg, North Carolina. He was in Signal Company. When Department of the Army shut down the 3rd Special Forces Group, its personnel were reassigned to a new brigade with the 101st Airborne Division that was being shipped to Vietnam. So Mike went to Vietnam.

I took a few days off from Kontum and went to visit my brother. When I arrived at his base camp, and finally found him, he was digging a hole for a urinal. Mike was at the bottom of a 10-foot-deep hole passing up a bucket of dirt to two other guys. He climbed out, we said our hellos, and then he and his friends placed stove pipe in the hole and filled it with crushed rock. Their task was finished. They all quit working and we went to their makeshift club. Mike and his two buddies were caught swimming at an off-limits watering hole, so their First Sergeant put them on a latrine detail. I arrived just as they were finishing their third urinal.
Mike was the more adventurous of the two Carden brothers. We spent a couple of days together and then I went back to Kontum.

The circumstances were a little different the next time I saw Mike. I was at My Phuoc Tay in the Mekong Delta and a message marked "URGENT" came in. My presence was requested at the 24th Evacuation Hospital, Long Binh, South Vietnam because my brother had been admitted as a patient. That's all the message said.

I travelled light. I took my CAR-15 and a rucksack with a change of clothes and food for a few days. I caught a helicopter to Saigon, borrowed a jeep from the Special Forces detachment at Saigon, and drove to the 24th Evac Hospital at Long Binh.

Mike's ward was the top of a "T" at the end of a corridor. When entering the ward, I was met by an MP with a shotgun. Mike's part of the ward was on the right side of the "T" and had patients from the 101st Airborne Division. The left side of the "T" had patients from the Military Confinement Facility across the street from the hospital. The reason for the guard.

There had been a race riot at the Long Binh Jail, the facility that was used to incarcerate soldiers who had been found guilty of serious crimes by court martial, and the seriously injured prisoners were treated and admitted to the hospital.

The 101st Airborne Division side of the ward had soldiers who were seriously wounded, except my brother. Mike had been incapacitated by kidney stones. So he was medevac'd to Long Binh. During the time I spent with him, I learned that Mike had no love lost for the Army and was looking forward to the day he could leave that part of his life in the past.

Because I knew how Mike felt about the Army, I was later surprised to learn that he had extended his tour in Vietnam by six months. When I called him through the Military switchboard, he told me that he would be released six months early from the Army if he extended his tour in Vietnam by six months. And, he didn't have to stay in the 101st Airborne Division. So he got a job as a door gunner on a Huey helicopter. He loved flying. Plus, he made a modification to the M-60 machine gun that was used on Hueys that was adopted by the Army for use on all gunships.

There's a saying that goes something like this: "If it's too good to be true, then it probably isn't." Mike's life of "milk runs" was short lived. His aviation unit was attached for duty to the 101st Airborne Division. Mike was shot down twice. And the third time, the pilot had been killed and he recovered the co-pilot. Mike left Vietnam a highly decorated hero…which he didn't want. The co-pilot of Mike's last mission spent many years and the remainder of his life in a VA hospital. Mike visited him often for many years. And as soon as he saw Mike, their conversations always started the same way: "Mike, what are you doing here?" His life-long friend was still in Vietnam.

After Vietnam, Mike married his high school sweetheart. They had two sons. But the demons from Vietnam wouldn't leave him alone. And eventually, they destroyed his marriage.

For many, many years Mike, along with thousands of other

Vietnam Veterans, fought the multi-layered bureaucracy of the Veterans Administration (VA) to get recognition and classification for Delayed Vietnam Stress Syndrome. Finally, the United States government recognized Post Traumatic Stress Disorder (PTSD) as a disability. Mike was classified 100% disabled.

Mike owned a houseboat and lived in Florida. Once in a while a hurricane would damage his home. He would get it fixed. Then, a hurricane came along that blew his houseboat nearly a half mile inland. It was time to live somewhere else. He moved to a little island off the coast of Panama. Twice a year, he would return to the States for a VA evaluation. Then he would go back to his home in Panama. Recently, Mike decided to take up a permanent residence in Florida. Family is now closer than a continent away.

CHRISTMAS EVE 1968

It was approximately 10:00 p.m. (2200) on Christmas Eve 1968. The place was the Mekong Delta in South Viet Nam. The night was very serene as I was sitting on top of a defensive bunker looking at the star-lit sky. In the distance to my front, an American soldier was firing red tracers across the horizon from my right to left. From the other direction, green tracers were travelling in a stream from my left to right.

Then there were other sets of red and green tracers interwoven in an arc as they were travelling from right to left and left to right. I do not believe either side was shooting at each other. They were making a beautiful red and green garland that arced in front of my position for about half an hour.

I think of that night every Christmas holiday season. It was the only Christmas in my lifetime that I recall with such clarity.

VC CHARLIE

VC Charlie was a recurring cartoon character in the Stars & Stripes. Story lines followed his trials and tribulations as he tried to be a good Viet Cong. One story line I distinctly remember lasted about a month. He was summoned to a munitions factory in Hanoi. When he arrived, he was given a mortar round and instructed to take it south.

So, travelling through a few cartoon panels a day, VC Charlie was off and running to get his mortar round to the mortar crew that was in dire need of it. He crossed raging rivers, underwent torrential downpours, survived attacks by ferocious jungle creatures, and circumvented enemy ambushes and B-52 airstrikes.

Bedraggled, he finally arrived at the mortar crew's location. VC Charlie handed the mortar to the ammunition bearer who dropped it down a mortar tube. There was a "Poof!" Then, VC Charlie was told to go get another one.

MASCOTS

I returned to Special Forces Team B-24 at Kontum in the early summer of 1969. I even got my old cot back. I was coming back to Kontum somewhat of a legend. My friends had told the NUGS (New Guys) stories that were probably 90% BS and 10% lies. And these kids believed it! I was the grizzled old Staff Sergeant coming into camp at the ripe old age of twenty-two. To the seasoned Senior Noncommissioned Officers, I was the nice young man or young kid who was moving up the ranks fast. It was time to make new friends.

This story is about Tom. Tom was a feline mascot. Tom was medium size, gold and brown with markings similar to tiger stripes. The new cinder block 403rd SOD Operations Bunker had a rat problem. At night, when it was closed and locked up, rats would scurry about and also eat the wiring of the electronic intelligence communications equipment. The electronic equipment repairmen were tired of fixing chewed up wiring. This was a mission for Tom.

One night when the building was being secured, the closing team left Tom inside the bunker with a bowl of food and some water. They went to bed. The next morning when the bunker was opened, Tom was sitting on his haunches at the entrance to the bunker. He was a mess. Tom was missing a few chunks of fur and it was obvious that he was in an all out battle. Lying around the bunker, under and on top of communications equipment, were about a half dozen large rats in various states of demise. That was the end of the rat infestation inside the bunker. Tom was placed into retirement and all he had to do was eat food, drink water and sleep.

This entry is about Bonnie & Clyde, a pair of white three-month-old short hair puppies that had been spared a Montangard stew pot at Dak To. They arrived at B-24 by helicopter mid-summer 1969. Bonnie & Clyde had the run of the camp and all of our Montangards knew that they were the Team Mascots.

The primary mission of the 403rd Special Operations Detachment (Airborne), 5th Special Forces Group (Airborne) was two-fold: Communications Intelligence (COMINT) & Analysis and Force Protection. In a nutshell: Keeping tabs on the enemy and telling the teams we supported where the enemy was located. There were a couple of ways to do this. Communications intercept & radio direction finding and boots on the ground. We were all very good at what we did. Not bragging, just a fact.

The primary source of Communications Intelligence was through Morse code intercept, analyzing communications patterns and tying everything together with radio direction finding. This mission was mostly accomplished at fixed locations; primarily the Special Forces camps located throughout Vietnam. A second source of Communications Intelligence was accompanying Special Forces Teams and Mike Force on reconnaissance and combat operations. These were LLVI missions (Low-level voice intercept); commonly referred to as hard wire taps. LLVIs were the most dangerous because once emplaced, you had to return to the same location to retrieve the data.

In an attempt to keep their communications somewhat secure, the North Vietnamese would string communications wire up to half a mile so their subordinate units could conduct voice communications. LLVI was an intelligence collection asset we used to tap into that valuable tactical intelligence source. It worked for a couple of years. Then the North Vietnamese started using wire-walkers to locate the hand emplaced devices. Then one of two things happened. Booby-traps were set or ambushes were emplaced. Either way, it wasn't a pleasant situation to walk into. So because of the unnecessary inherent danger associated with LLVI, these missions were terminated after two years of success.

By supporting several different Special Forces Teams in the Central Highlands and the Mekong Delta; and occasionally going on missions with Mike Force, I made many life-long friends who themselves were years later in positions of authority within the Special Forces community. It made my job much easier in later years, when I was a Team Sergeant and later Operations Sergeant, to send people to my friends' Special Forces units to support their training exercises and white missions overseas.

Circa Mid-Summer 1969. Charlie was a Sergeant First Class. As I write this, it irritates me to no end that I can't remember his last name. I knew it when I went to the Wall in 1985, and now, twenty four years later, I don't remember. I remember his laugh and that for some reason his trousers were always ripped when he came out of the jungle. We used to play hearts and spades at camp to pass the time.

I was accompanying his team and a company of Montangards in Kontum Province in the Central Highlands of Vietnam. Also accompanying Charlie's team was an Australian Special Forces guy. In our travels through the jungle, I had emplaced a hard-tap on a North Vietnamese communications wire. Either I or someone else would retrieve the recordings a couple of weeks later.

This foray into the jungle was uneventful. We had been out four days and were waiting in the tree line at the edge of our Landing Zone to be picked up by helicopters. Hueys and Chinooks would be coming in. As the helicopters came in and landed, Charlie, the Australian Special Forces guy and I headed briskly through two-foot high elephant grass toward a Huey. When we reached the Huey, we tossed our rucksacks onto the floor. Charlie dropped to the ground. The Australian guy and I picked him up and put him on the helicopter. Being under the rotor blade, we didn't hear any gun fire. The door gunner sprayed the tree line with his M-60 30-caliber machine gun, but there were no enemy forces visible. It took about twenty minutes to return to Kontum. Charlie had died instantly when the bullet hit him in the back and pierced his heart.

Newsreel footage of U.S. Forces in Vietnam is primarily of conventional units. The Army and Marines wore sixteen-pound protective vests to protect the torso and a WWII vintage steel helmet to protect the head. Special Forces didn't wear steel pots or protective vests. They were readily available for camp defense, but too cumbersome in the field.

I've only been to the Wall once and that was to say goodbye to Charlie from Ohio. I never knew he was from Ohio, but the directory at the Wall lists people by their Name, Rank, Home State of Record and Date of Death.

Kontum Charlie. This is the nickname we gave to a Viet Cong observer who was providing intelligence about American activities and movements to Viet Cong and North Vietnamese forces in the vicinity of Kontum, Vietnam. He made regular reports to his higher headquarters and we knew his approximate location was within 250 meters of Special Forces Camp B24. It was just a matter of finding him.

I was outside the wire about 6:00 pm and returning to camp when I heard an AM radio transmitter tuning. The faint sound was coming from a Vietnamese house about 100 meters from our front gate. I went to the S-2 (Intelligence Officer) and he put together a team to go get the observer. The house was surrounded; we entered and captured him without incident. The Viet Cong observer had buried his coaxial cable and was using a portion of our perimeter fence as a radio antenna. He was quite resourceful.

Nha Trang Charlie. I was called to Nha Trang to help out the Air Force. Nha Trang Charlie was a thorn in their side. I worked with a team from the 6994th Air Force Security Squadron and Nha Trang Charlie's location was determined to be near a huge boulder on the side of the mountain overlooking Nha Trang and the American Army, Navy and Air Force facilities. The Air Force Base was taking the brunt of Viet Cong intrusions. Project Delta, the predecessor to Delta Force, went in and captured him.

CHICOM. I was sent from Nha Trang to Dak To, a Special Forces camp in Kontum Province. Unconfirmed reports surfaced that placed CHICOM (Chinese Communist) military advisors in the surrounding area. I spent two months at Dak To looking for the Chinese and came up with nothing. It doesn't mean they weren't there, I just couldn't find them.

Circa 1969. Conventional units periodically would come to Kontum. Since the Ho Chi Minh Trail ran past us, conventional units would engage the enemy, claim a high body count, and leave.

Then one day the 4th ID (Infantry Division) showed up. Their main element was on the other side of Kontum across the river. They had a few M60 Main Battle Tanks and a lot of APCs (M113 Armored Personnel Carrier). I'm guessing they had a battalion of MPs (Military Police) with all the MPs that were running around. MPs set up road blocks, rode around in jeeps, had walking beats in Kontum itself, and they carried ticket books for traffic citations.

My friend Toby went over to the 4th ID because he wanted to drive an APC. He had never driven one before and wanted to give it a try. So he drove over to their tent city and parked his jeep at the motor pool, walked inside, climbed into an APC, started it up and drove around for a while. Then he parked it, got back into his jeep and returned to B24.

One afternoon, I was returning to camp after picking up some sand bags at the river. I had about 10 filled sand bags in the back of my jeep. I drove through Kontum and was at the edge of town and the rest of my trip home was about a half mile stretch to the B24 gate. I encountered an MP road block. I stopped my jeep and asked what was going on. The MP told me it was a vehicle safety check and he wanted to see my military driver's license. I said, "Excuse me?" I explained to him that we didn't carry military driver's licenses and I didn't have time for a safety check and that I had to go. He was reaching for his ticket book when I said, "Adios." I put my jeep in gear and headed down the road toward camp. Two MPs hopped in a jeep and were right behind me. In case they got stupid, at least I knew I had sand bags piled behind the driver's seat. The Montangard guards saw me coming and opened the gate. The guard on the .50 caliber machine gun locked and loaded. I stopped my jeep inside the compound and walked back to the gate. The MP came up to the gate and I said, "See, my jeep runs fine. The wheels didn't fall off and the brakes worked when I needed them. Now as far as a license, I probably have one, but I haven't seen it in a couple of years." He started to quote a 4th Infantry Division regulation and I said, "I'm not in the 4th Infantry Division. Why don't you and your buddy come on in and I'll buy you a beer in our club and we'll call it a day."

The two MPs drove into the compound and followed me the short distance to our club. When we went inside, I rolled down the sleeves on my jungle fatigues and they saw my rank. The MP said, "Why didn't you identify yourself as a Staff Sergeant?" I asked why. He said that their instructions were to pass through officers and NCOs and only do safety checks of vehicles driven by junior people. I told him then they need to take their road blocks back across the river because nobody on our compound was below the rank of Sergeant. As a matter of fact, most of the people in the camp were Senior NCOs. I also told him that inside the gate we were all equals and he and his buddies could come over any time they wanted. The club would always be open for them. That little encounter had generated new revenue for our club.

The MP turned out to be an all right guy. He and his friends came over regularly. The MPs still had road blocks, but not on our side of the river.

Law and order was running rampant. One day I had to cross the river to go to the 4th ID Military Intelligence unit. After business was concluded, I started my return trip back to camp. Before reaching the MP check point at the bridge, there was an accident. An M60 Main Battle Tank had thrown a tread and veered off the road hitting a Vietnamese house. The tank was parked in what used to be the living room. An MP was writing a traffic ticket to give to the tank driver. It must have been for illegal parking.

Circa 1969. September or October. Special Forces Camp B-24, Kontum, Viet Nam. Periodically, we would make a courier run to our next higher headquarters at Pleiku, Viet Nam. The purpose of the courier runs was to transport hard copies of low-level tactical intelligence. My boss, Sergeant First Class Robert B. Courchaine, selected me as the jeep driver. A clerk who was from the MACV compound (Military Assistance Command Viet Nam) was looking for a ride to Pleiku. He wanted to take a break from his clerking duties. The route to Pleiku was for the most part under American and South Vietnamese Army control. There weren't any major North Vietnamese Army units in the area, but there were smaller Viet Cong elements, and it was always best to be prepared in case anything should happen. So Bob tossed the clerk an M-79 Grenade Launcher and told him that if we ran into trouble to pop off a couple of rounds. The clerk was excited that he may see some "action."

The actual trip would take about an hour. Once on the two-lane hard-packed red clay road, it would be pedal to the metal. After passing through Kontum, I approached a Vietnamese Army checkpoint at the river crossing outside of Kontum proper. I pulled up to the sandbagged guard position and was waved through by the guard. I crossed the two-lane metal trestle bridge which spanned a 150 meter wide river. Once across the bridge, it was no man's land for about 20 miles. There were occasional thatched roof houses along the road in which Vietnamese families lived. Behind the houses were groupings of rice paddies that spanned an area of about 200 meters to the tree line. One mile down the road, I was stopped by a 4th Infantry Division Military Police roadblock. Only groups of two or more vehicles were allowed to pass for the travelers' safety and security. Two jeeps came up from CCC (Command and Control Central, a special element of Special Forces, sort of a predecessor to Delta Force). There were three Command and Control elements in Viet Nam; CCC, CCS and CCN-Central, South and North.

The CCC compound was located near the river outside Kontum. They operated independently and would go on cross-border missions into Cambodia, Laos and North Vietnam. Their missions included sabotage at enemy munitions depots and covert operations inside enemy encampments. They were unique and it took a special type of person with nerves of steel to do the job they were tasked to perform.

Bob spoke with the CCC guys for a couple of minutes and we were off with our jeep bringing up the rear. About half way to Pleiku there was an air strike in progress to our right front about 150 meters off the road on the tree line. The plane was a Vietnamese Sky Raider (A-1 attack bomber used primarily by the U.S. Navy) and he had dropped a couple of small bombs and flew away. The bombs were probably 200 pounds because they only made a small KAWHOOM and blew dirt in all directions. It wasn't clear what the bomber was attacking on the tree line, but it was an indication there was some type of enemy force in the area. As we came abreast of the site where the air strike had taken place, we came under intense AK-47 automatic rifle fire. The AK-47 has a very distinctive sound. There is no other weapon in the world that sounds like it. Not a very pleasant feeling being on the receiving end of one.

All three vehicles pulled over to the right and we instinctively took up defensive positions in the adjacent ditch that had about a three-foot high embankment. The four CCC guys were together on the left and Bob, the clerk and I were on the right. We returned fire into the tree line. As usual, when engaged in a firefight, the participants return fire toward the location from where it comes. Very seldom in combat do you actually see your adversary when he is in a defensive position. While we were firing, Bob told the clerk to pop some rounds down range with the grenade launcher. The M-79 is a single shot grenade launcher. It is reloaded by flicking a lever and opening the breech in the same manner you would open a shotgun, inserting a grenade round, closing the breech, and firing. This process is repeated until you're finished or you run out of grenade rounds. We had a nice little firefight going and I was closest to the CCC guys. One of them said, "Let's rush them." Now, we're firing automatic weapons at the Viet Cong, and they're firing automatic weapons at us. We have very good protection behind a dirt berm that separates us from 150 meters of open ground that terminates at a tree line that conceals a bunch of other guys wearing black pajamas shooting at us. "Rushing" a concealed, fortified defensive position didn't make a whole lot of sense to me. I was trying to think of a diplomatic way to say they should reconsider when I blurted out, "Are you f**kin' nuts?" I don't typically use this type of language and struggled with putting it in this story, but that's the way it was.

It was a moot issue. At that exact moment, a Vietnamese Army APC (Armored Personnel Carrier) with a .50 caliber machine gun turned off the road and went up and over the embankment heading toward the tree line with its machine gun blazing away. The APC had considerably more fire power than we did and was better equipped to handle the situation. There was nothing to do except get back into our Jeeps and continue our trip to Pleiku. The remainder of the ride to Pleiku was uneventful. However, Bob and I had to listen to the excited ranting of the clerk who just had his first combat experience. I never saw those CCC guys again. We had heard stories about Command and Control guys' exploits and how gung-ho they were, but had previously chalked them up to folklore. The proof is in the pudding. The CCC guys lived up to the hype we had heard about them. Leave unicorns for folklore, the CCC guys were the real thing.

Nicknames are bestowed upon people for various and assundry reasons as a result of an event, action or assumption. When I was a kid, my Dad tagged me with "Eucalyptus" because I missed the word in a spelling bee. (I was the 1958 Dodge County Nebraska Spelling Bee Champion and missed a shot at nationals). Recently, I watched the National Spelling Bee on TV and I don't believe that I would have gotten past the first commercial.

In the Military, nicknames are for the most part, a reflection on the individual.

The best soldier I ever met was nicknamed FROSTY. This was a take on his name, which was Clovis D. Ice. Command Sergeant Major Clovis D. Ice was without doubt the best Senior Noncommissioned Officer in the United States Army. He was highly regarded from Private through General Officer. FROSTY was also one of the nicest guys in the world. Through all the years I knew him, he always had a smile and never raised his voice in anger. He was my Sergeant Major in Viet Nam in the late 1960's. He was a good friend in the 1970's. After CSM Ice retired, he was the law enforcement official in a small North Carolina town. He stopped by my unit a few times to chat. He wore his police uniform. The first time he was a Sergeant. Next, he was a Captain. The last time I saw him, he had all kinds of gold braid on his police uniform. He told me he made himself Chief of Police. Frosty unexpectedly died as a result of Agent Orange. He was inducted into the U.S. Army Military Intelligence Hall of Fame and his portrait is displayed at the U.S. Army Intelligence School, Fort Huachuca, Arizona.

Sergeant First Class Eddie Hiett was LITTLE DIRNSA. The nickname was a take on the Director, National Security Agency. Eddie Hiett was, without doubt, the most technically proficient soldier in his chosen career field in the United States Army. He excelled at Morse code and Morse communications analysis. I learned technical skills from him my first year in Viet Nam that would normally take a career to accumulate.

My nickname was WRONGDOER. Frosty gave it to me the first time I met him in an official capacity. As a young lad, I had a tendency not to follow orders to the letter of the law. I had been called to Nha Trang, 5th Special Forces Group Headquarters, Viet Nam for an award ceremony. It seems I was getting a Bronze Star. I had disobeyed an order, maybe a little harsh, I ignored an order given by an officer and did something that resulted in the recommendation. I received a promotion and the award at the same time. That's when I made the determination that if you do something wrong in the Army, they'll either court martial you or promote you and give you a medal.

BOOM-BOOM GAS CAN. I always had the impression the holder of this dubious nickname didn't much care for it. The nickname itself was bestowed upon its owner because of an incident during his assignment in Panama before going to Viet Nam. There was an explosion in the motor pool and rumor was he was the person responsible for said explosion. Deserved or not, the nickname was his during his Military career.

LYIN' SLY CY BENNETT. I first met Cy after I had been in Viet Nam a couple of years. He was considerably older than the rest of us. As a matter of fact, he was older than dirt. Cy was a teller of tall tales. He had the ability to look anyone in the eye and speak an untruth. It was a treat listening to him spin a yarn.

CLANK. Staff Sergeant John Norwood was a good friend to everyone. He smoked a pipe and was always available for sage advice. John could have had a medical retirement as a young soldier. He wore braces and could have had a deferment from duty in Viet Nam. His dedication to duty wouldn't allow it. John retired after serving his country for 20 years. Somewhere along the line, his nickname changed to IRONMAN, maybe in deference to his age. I can still visualize and hear clank, clank, clank as he was walking or running.

BIG KAHUNA. Command Sergeant Major (Retired) James A. Smith III. Our careers paralleled each other. Jim is Hawaiian, six feet two inches tall, 240 pounds and the smallest of three brothers. Jim is one of my two best friends, two months younger than me and still competes in martial arts tournaments, and is serving his community today as a high school teacher in Pennsylvania.

QUICKDRAW MCSTALEY. Gun collector. A take on the "Quickdraw McGraw" cartoon character. At any given time, he would have no less than three concealed weapons on his person. One memorable encounter was when he produced a small pistol from his concealed fly holster.

DIRTY GARY WEESE. Nothing to do with hygiene. With Gary, it was win at any cost. He was unmatched at combat volleyball. Gary had a tendency to play dirty. And he won.

TOBY. Nothing special, Toby is his name. But, his sister is special. Toby's sister worked for Playboy Magazine. She modeled products. Each issue a body part belonging to Toby's sister would be in the magazine. One month would be her eyes, another her hands, her legs and so forth. It would take years to get a complete picture of her.

I had other friends like CLANK who were either held together by metal or had replacement parts and refused medical retirements. Today's generation of soldiers is like them. There are some who are remaining on Active Duty after severe injuries and returning to Iraq and Afghanistan. I get weekly accounts of these American Heroes in my Military periodicals.

From my Viet Nam days, there was a guy we all knew and all stayed away from. No one dared make eye contact with him. He could freeze water with a glance. This man was a decorated hero from the Korean War and had been a POW. He was impervious to pain. He didn't have a nickname. I'm not sure if anyone knew his real name. He didn't want friends and we didn't impose.

RANGER JOE

Joseph D. Byrne was from New Jersey and he was a Ranger. His Dad was in state politics and was either the governor or a state senator. The first time I met Joe, he was a member of the recruiting team that did the initial testing before I was accepted for Special Forces. Joe was a Sergeant and I was a Private First Class. After I was assigned to the 403rd Special Operations Detachment, 3rd Special Forces Group, Fort Bragg, North Carolina we became good friends. We went to Viet Nam together. I only saw Joe a few times during his time in country and we lost touch for several years after he left Viet Nam.

We ran into each other once when I was a First Sergeant and Joe was an Army Recruiter. Joe retired near Fort Devens, Massachusetts. I always thought he would enter into politics. Instead, he opened an insurance agency and his wife went into politics. She was at one time a Massachusetts state senator.

Master Sergeant Joseph D. Byrne retired after a twenty-year distinguished Military career. Distinguished Soldier, American Hero, Deceased.

My Mentors

This story is about my mentors. First, there were my Detachment Sergeants Major. As an 18-year-old Private First Class, my very first Sergeant Major was Walter Britton. He went to Viet Nam with us on the U.S.S. General George Weigel. My next Sergeant Major was Clovis D. Ice, "Frosty," who many have considered the most respected man in the United States Army. He was a mentor to me throughout my Military career, even after he retired. Frosty was inducted into the Military Intelligence Hall of Fame upon his retirement. These two men made a huge impression on me and were the driving force behind how I conducted myself throughout my Military career.

Sergeant First Class Eddie Hiett was the first person to teach me, in detail, the technical side of my Military Intelligence skills. Our primary specialty was in Communications Intelligence (COMINT), and each Service had a unique branch dedicated to this field. The United States Navy is purported to have the best technicians. However, not a Sailor on this planet could match the skills of Eddie Hiett. He was the best in the Department of Defense and my fellow Soldiers and I were quite fortunate to have him as a teacher. The technical skills I learned from him in one short year would take others several years to learn through many diversified assignments.

Sergeant First Class Al Fauber was my next mentor. What I learned from Al was to stand up for what is right and to not take any guff from anyone, regardless of who they were or who they thought they were. Another thing I learned from Al was that we were family and nobody outside our circle messed with our family. When Al was my boss, I was a 20-year-old Sergeant. Throughout my career, I didn't allow anyone to run roughshod over any of my people and I had a reputation for supporting the underdog. Once, when I was a Sergeant First Class, a Senior Noncommissioned Officer, I interceded on behalf of a young soldier who was being unduly chastised by a Lieutenant Colonel who was a Battalion Commander and the Airborne Commander on a night administrative parachuting operation. We had a rather heated discussion and the last thing he said to me was, "That's my opinion Sergeant and nothing will change it." His opinion was changed when the 5th Special Forces Group Commander relieved him of his command and he was reassigned out of Special Forces.

Sergeant First Class Robert B. Courchaine was Al's replacement and took me under his wing. He was the hardest on me. Whatever I did, it could have been done better. He was a tough task master. He instilled in me my work ethic. "It ain't over till it's over." Bob was my last leader in Viet Nam. I had just under three and a half years in-country and I was going home. With less than two months left, I planned on taking it easy and just sort of slipping unnoticed out of Viet Nam. The early morning of December 1st, 1969, Bob woke me up, told me to grab my stuff and meet him on the helipad. We were going to the Tumerong Valley. I said, "No, I'm not!" As I was jumping off the helicopter into elephant grass under hostile fire from a North Vietnamese Regimental Command Post, I thought I was making my position very clear that I did not want to be there. My protests fell upon deaf ears. During the ten days we were in the valley, we lost ten Americans. Firebase Foxtrot became somewhat of a legend in Military history. In a short period of time, there were numerous selfless acts of heroism from a small group of American Soldiers in a place unknown to anyone. Bob recovered the crewmembers from a downed helicopter, and for that selfless act under fire, he was later decorated for heroism. Bob and I faced death together. Two weeks after action in the Tumerong, Bob's tour of duty was over and he returned to the States. I departed Viet Nam in early February 1970, went home for a month and reported in to the 402nd Special Operations Detachment, 10th Special Forces Group, Fort Devens, Massachusetts. Sergeant First Class Courchaine was once again my Team Sergeant and I was one of the leaders of a subordinate team. Bob taught me night land navigation by using the stars and moon, the Transverse Mercator System, and how to determine your daytime location from an unknown when the only tools you have are a Military lensatic compass, a blank sheet of paper, and a pencil.

Sergeant First Class T.C. Bunn taught me never to let my guard down. Always expect the unexpected. Through the luck of the draw, I got T.C. as a sparring partner when testing for my black belt in Tae Kwon Do. We were in Thailand and karate was full contact. No gloves, protective gear or mats. All matches were on a hard teak floor. My instructor had been working with me one-on-one for a month in preparation for my test. He said I was ready. The question was, "Was T.C. ready for me?" The first half minute was more or less tit for tat. I saw my opening and took it. T.C. countered. I spent the next few days hobbling around on crutches.

President Ronald Reagan. He wasn't a mentor, but I was duly impressed when I got to meet him in early 1981. After my successfully completing my tour of duty with the Central Intelligence Agency and the successful mission working the plane hijacking of PK147 at Rawalpindi, Pakistan, some people at Langley set up the meeting. The meeting itself was only a few seconds, but for me it lasted a lifetime.

President George Herbert Walker Bush. Another person who wasn't a mentor, but I was impressed by the man. The Commander, Southern Command bestowed upon me the responsibility of ensuring that nothing happened to the President during his official visit to Panama. No problem. Everything went well, I got a medal, and when the Honduran Minister of Defense came to Panama, he asked for me.

My Mom and Dad. They instilled in me core values and a sense of right and wrong. Everything I am, I owe to them.

As I was one of the original members of the Fort Bragg SOD, Bob was an original member of the Germany SOD. I first met Bob when the troop transport I was on docked at Okinawa enroute to Vietnam. The Okinawa SOD had come to meet us and be our hosts for the six hours we would be on the island. Bob invited some of my friends and me to his home and we had dinner with his family. It was a fun time. Others had fun of a different sort. They were introduced to Saki and Okinawan beer and the remainder of their trip was hanging over the guard rail of the USS General George Weigel for the next two days.

I had been in Vietnam for two and a half years when our paths crossed again. Sergeant First Class Robert B. Courchaine was assigned to Kontum and he was my boss after I returned from the Mekong Delta. During his assignment in the Central Highlands, we had become life-long friends. After Vietnam, Bob was Best Man at my wedding and our wives were best friends. I am Godfather to his son as he is Godfather to mine. The bond we have was formed in war.

He watched my back as I watched his. Bob had this thing about helicopters; Huey UH1D's in particular. Whenever he got on one, it crashed. The first time was unfortunate. The second time was coincidence. The third time people started wondering. The fourth time, people watched to see which helicopter Bob got on and they opted for another. I showed my support for Bob, but buckled in tight. That chopper had engine trouble and didn't get off the ground. Spell breaking happens in fives.

I was in Vietnam nearly three years and finishing my final tour. A term all soldiers used was "short." It meant you were going home and the war was over for you. There were associations with the term also. "I'm so short, I have to climb a ladder to jump off a nickel." There were people who sandbagged their beds for protection while they slept. I had about 60 days left. I let it be known that I was not leaving camp until I got on a helicopter to go to Saigon to get on a Freedom Bird to go home. Nobody listened.

01 December 1969. Before daybreak, Bob woke me up, told me to grab my stuff and meet him on the helipad. We were going to the Tumerong Valley. I said, "No, I'm not!" As I was jumping off a

helicopter into elephant grass right in the middle of a North Vietnamese Regimental Command Post, I was contemplating the meaning of life, in particular, mine. I tried to impress upon Bob that short timers don't do this, but to no avail. As I think about our foray into the valley, it reminds me of "Apocalypse Now" and helicopters flying to music over the horizon like a swarm of bees.

We were now officially Firebase Foxtrot. This was a joint operation with Vietnamese Rangers at one end of the valley; Vietnamese Infantry at the other end of the valley; and us, American Special Forces and Vietnamese Artillery with two American advisors, and a company of Montangard Civilian Irregular Defense Group (CIDG—Special Forces-trained infantry). The incursion began with a massive surprise helicopter assault on a North Vietnamese Regimental Headquarters. The assault caught them off guard and we had the advantage for the first half of the operation. However, the Vietnamese Infantry and Rangers at the north and south ends of the valley were no match for the North Vietnamese soldiers and it ended up with 20-25 Americans in a force of approximately 200 holding off a regiment in the center of the valley. Our resupplies were ammunition. Helicopters would fly in low, drop sling loads of artillery canister rounds and small arms ammunition as we provided cover fire. We lost one of the helicopters on the last day and it went down behind enemy lines. Bob led a rescue mission to the helicopter and brought back the remains of the crew. There is a standing rule in the Military. No one is left behind. Ten will sacrifice themselves to save one. That is the underlying camaraderie that complete strangers have for each other. It's not patriotism, the flag, or Mom's apple pie, but the person next to you.

Ten days of two opposing forces trying to decide who would keep a little piece of ground. Our 105 howitzers were set up in a circle like a wagon train from the Old West and aimed straight ahead firing canister rounds. We lost ten Americans in ten days. Bob was later decorated for heroism, as were the American artillery advisors and all the other Special Forces soldiers. We went into the valley under fire and we left the same way.

As a young lad, Bob was mischievous, really a juvenile delinquent. Nothing dishonest, just mischievous. Rolling car tires down hills in town or riding the bumper of a city transit bus. Fun stuff. He was, and still is, a good family man. Bob was one of my mentors as well as the mentor for several other soldiers through the years. Master Sergeant Robert B. Courchaine retired from the United States Army in 1978 after serving his Nation honorably for twenty years.

A final note. In the early fall of 1970, the 402nd Special Operations Detachment from Fort Devens, Massachusetts was participating in a Field Training Exercise (FTX) with the Special Warfare Center at Fort Bragg, North Carolina. Bob and I were on a mountain in the Uhwarrie National Forest for two weeks. We spent the whole time talking about getting a tattoo. When we returned to Fort Bragg and headed into Fayetteville, North Carolina, we went directly to a tattoo emporium. As we entered, a Marine was getting a Bulldog on his forearm and tears were streaming down his cheeks. I was having second thoughts. "Next!" Bob said to go ahead, he was still deciding. I opted for a parachutist badge topped by SF for Special Forces on my outside left bicep. When I was finished, I asked Bob what he was getting. Bob said, "I changed my mind."

The Soldier's Medal is awarded for heroism not involving contact with the enemy. It involves risking your life to save the lives of others. Criteria must meet or exceed that required for award of the Distinguished Flying Cross (DFC); or as in my case, meet criteria for award of the Distinguished Service Cross (DSC).

Following is the Department of the Army general order:

DEPARTMENT OF THE ARMY
Headquarters, United States Army Vietnam
APO San Francisco 96375

GENERAL ORDERS NUMBER 534   26 February 1970

AWARD OF THE SOLDIER'S MEDAL

TC 439.   The following AWARD is announced.

CARDEN, DAVID C. (SSAN) STAFF SERGEANT United States Army, Detachment B-24, Company B, 5th Special Forces Group (Airborne), 1st Special Forces, APO 96499

Awarded: Soldier's Medal
Date of action: 2 December 1969
Theater: Republic of Vietnam
Authority: By direction of the President, under the provisions of the Act of Congress, approved 2 July 1926.

Reason: For heroism not involving actual conflict with an armed enemy in the Republic of Vietnam: Staff Sergeant Carden distinguished himself on 2 December 1969 while serving at Firebase Foxtrot in the Central Highlands of the Republic of Vietnam. As a helicopter was landing in the compound that morning, the downdraft from its rotor blades fanned the cooking fire of a Vietnamese gun crew out of control. The fire spread rapidly over a dry, grassy area and into a nearby ammunition storage area igniting 105-millimeter howitzer charges and bandoliers of small arms ammunition. Realizing that if the fire were not quickly contained, high explosive 105-millimeter artillery rounds stored in the area would soon ignite, Sergeant Carden rushed into the ammunition dump amid bursting small arms ammunition and flying debris and began beating out the flames with a shovel. Once the blaze had been brought under control, Sergeant Carden removed the high explosive artillery rounds to a safer location. Sergeant Carden's efforts in bringing the fire under control were instrumental in preventing the loss of life and equipment that would have resulted had the high explosive ammunition ignited. Staff Sergeant Carden's heroic actions were in keeping with the highest traditions of the military service and reflect great credit upon himself, his unit, and the United States Army.

GEORGE L. MABRY, JR.
Major General, US Army
Chief of Staff

FOR THE COMMANDER:

JOHN A. O'BRIEN
Colonel, AGC
Adjutant General

The Certificate of Award was signed by the Adjutant General, Department of the Army and the Secretary of the Army.

AGENT ORANGE

I was recently scanning the Special Forces Association website and clicked on a link to B-24, the Special Forces camp at Kontum, Vietnam. I then found a link to a unit in the 4th Infantry Division that displayed photos of the area in and around Kontum. I recognized most of the locations in the photographs. Then I linked to an Air Force C-123 unit that sprayed defoliant on the jungle. There was a map showing dispersion of Agent Orange throughout South Vietnam. During the war, of all the provinces in South Vietnam, Kontum was sprayed more than any other; about four-and-a-half times more. Kontum Province received 910,415 gallons of Agent Orange sprayed on the countryside. The closest amount sprayed on any other province was a little over 200,000 gallons.

Writing this, I can still smell the pungent odor and see the dead foliage. Through the years, seven friends have died as a result of exposure to Agent Orange.

MORTALITY

We live, we die. Life goes on. That's the way it is. Remorse for fallen comrades ebbs over time. The one thing about life and death that has always bothered me is that life is fleeting and death is random.

There isn't a day that passes, or a night of peaceful sleep, that I don't think of comrades in arms who died. Not so much how they died; I don't dwell on that. What really bothers me is what they had planned for that day, week, month or rest of their lives.

One minute we're here, the next we cease to exist. I think of Frosty and Charlie and Tommy and George and Joe and TC and Ranger Joe and the people being carried out of the jungle in a poncho stretcher and how much they contributed and how much more they could have contributed.

Those who die are missed and honored by family, friends and a grateful nation.

The cycle continues. Life is fleeting, death is random.

Bud Oetgen and Arlis Oetgen (pronounced oat-jen) were my Mom and Dad's best friends. Bud was also a cross-country truck driver like my Dad; and Arlis was my Mom's best friend. Bud and Arlis didn't have children, and my siblings and I were sort of their surrogate kids. The adults would play cards or board games and we children would watch television or play board games ourselves with Monopoly being the most popular.

This story is more about Bud and how I respected him. Bud was a Veteran of WWII. Bud was Airborne. Bud was a Ranger. Bud was of German descent. Bud parachuted into Germany. Bud spent three years in a German Prisoner of War camp.

When I shipped out for Viet Nam and said goodbye to my family, I also said goodbye to Bud and Arlis. They wrote letters to me as often as my own family did. When I returned home, Bud and Arlis were also there to greet me.

The uniform issued to me after I left Viet Nam was the Winter Dress Green wool uniform. Naturally, about two sizes too big for me; although, today it would probably be two sizes too small. My Mother and Arlis took the uniform and performed alterations. After they were finished, I had a custom-made Dress Green Uniform that I had for many years afterward.

The first time I wore my newly altered uniform, I had all the ribbons and badges on it that were issued to me at the San Francisco embarkation point. I was wearing my brand new Green Beret, and blousing rubbers secured my trouser legs over the top of my paratrooper boots.

There were two WWII Veterans present. My Dad, who had been a tail gunner and later a straight-leg Infantryman; and Bud, who was the Airborne Ranger. Bud went ballistic. He stressed the importance of having pride in your uniform and under no circumstances does a Paratrooper ever wear sissy blousing rubbers. Trouser legs are tucked neatly into and bloused evenly over the tops of paratrooper boots. I never forgot that on-the-spot correction, and never for the remainder of my Military career, did I ever own another pair of blousing rubbers.

Circa 1970. Fort Devens, Massachusetts. After Viet Nam, some of my friends and I were assigned to the 402nd Special Operations Detachment (Airborne), 10th Special Forces Group (Airborne). We all needed transportation and bought new cars that suited our needs.

The married guys were already locked into sedans and station wagons; except my best friend Bob.

Bob had a full-size two-tone faded red and grayish white color manual four-speed Volkswagen bus. It was a remnant of his prior assignment in Germany.

Since this is my story, I'll start with me. WRONGDOER bought a 1970 Mustang convertible with dark green gold specked paint, white top, white leather interior, wood trim, four-speed automatic transmission and a V8 351 engine.

BIG KAHUNA bought a dark green Road Runner. I think he got it up to Mach 2. He always liked speed. Even when driving a jeep, he would push it to the limit.

QUICKDRAW bought a pale blue VW Beetle. I think it was to maintain a low profile.

George bought a blinding bright yellow Corvette. For some reason, George never had a nickname, but his car and girl friend did. Once he drove over a McDonald's paper bag and it knocked his oil pan off. Seems there was a rock inside the bag. So, after his oil pan was repaired, George placed the rock on his dashboard as an ornament.

How I Met Miss Elkhart

Circa 1970. Early summer. I had driven from Fort Devens, Massachusetts to attend a family function at my home in Fremont, Nebraska. Afterwards, I started my return trip to Fort Devens. It would take about two days. I drove 534 miles and wrapped my new Mustang convertible around a highway department truck at milepost 100.7 on the Indiana Toll Road at Elkhart, Indiana.

It was one of those 75 mph slow-motion things. I was in the right lane, came upon a parked gray truck that sort of blended into the roadway, turned hard to the left, and took off the right side of my car. I was wearing sun glasses, they flipped up, and my head hit the steering wheel, grinding glass into my forehead. There was a lot of blood, but it didn't hurt, and I was trying not to get blood on my white leather bucket seats. I unbuckled my seatbelt, stood up, and walked across the passenger side and exited my car where the door used to be. Milepost 100.7 was lying in my back seat.

I was transported to the hospital, some people cleaned up my face and bandaged my forehead, I took care of some administrative paperwork, and I exited the hospital and sat down at a bus stop. A nurse came up to me and asked where I was going. I told her I was going to find some place to stay for a couple of days. She told me that she was in the emergency room when they brought me in, that we had a lengthy conversation which I didn't remember, and that I was going home with her. So, I walked to the parking lot with her, got in her car and we went to her house where I met her younger brother and her parents. They were a really nice family.

The next day, I called my Sergeant Major and told him I would be returning a little later than planned. I went to where my car had been towed, removed all my personal items, and then met an insurance adjuster. He said my car would be totaled. The nurse, whose name was Barbara, took me to the local Ford dealership. I said I wanted another car exactly like mine. Ain't gonna happen. The insurance company approved a Mustang Boss 302 fastback as a replacement vehicle. I said no. I either get an exact replica or they could put my car back together. My car was scheduled for repair.

The next day, I thanked Barbara and her family for their hospitality.

Barbara drove me to the airport and I flew back to Massachusetts. That summer, I returned to Elkhart a couple of times. The first time was to see Barbara, and of course, her family. The second time was to pick up my rebuilt 1970 Mustang convertible which probably cost the insurance company twice as much to fix than what I paid for it. The repairs took a couple of months because there had been an auto parts strike. Although I wrecked my car, I'll always have fond memories of that summer in 1970. Barbara was Miss Elkhart. And my friend.

Circa 1970. Late December. This is when I met Miss Gracemary Ingemi. She was employed by the Fitchburg Fire Insurance Company, Fitchburg, Massachusetts. Gracemary was in charge of claims and it was her decision as to whether they were accepted.

Gracemary had four younger siblings. She was 22 years old and her siblings were 20, 17, 13 and 8 years old. Her Father was a successful businessman and her Mother was a homemaker.

Gracemary was the big city girl and I was the country boy. So why not get married? We were married on May 1st, 1971. It was supposed to be a year later but I received assignment orders to Panama with a reporting date of June 1st, 1971. So the wedding was rescheduled for May 1st, 1971. My parents couldn't attend the wedding because my sister at home was getting married on the same date. So after Gracemary and I were married, we drove out to Nebraska so my family could meet my new bride. We spent a week in Fremont, Nebraska and then returned to Massachusetts.

Gracemary's name was entered into my Military records as my next-of-kin and she went through all the processes for her dependent identification card, passport, survivor benefits, emergency contact numbers, and all the stuff soldiers' wives have to do. She also received her inoculations for traveling to Central America. She took everything like a trooper. Then my assignment orders for Panama were cancelled.

Gracemary kept her job with the insurance company. Looking back, I'm glad she did. Her weekly paycheck was more than what I made in a month as a Staff Sergeant. Gracemary's office was on the ground floor of a five story building in downtown Fitchburg, Massachusetts. The upper floors were apartments for elderly tenants, except us. We had an apartment on the third floor. So I ended up being the person our neighbors called whenever they couldn't find something or needed assistance. I didn't mind, they were nice people. I think the octogenarian ladies were flirting with me. Late one morning there was a knock on our door. When we answered, we were told our neighbor across the hall hadn't been seen recently and people were concerned. So, I knocked on her door and there was no answer. A couple more knocks and still no answer. I went out onto the balcony, inched my way across the side of the building to an open window, and entered her apartment. I called out her name and there was no answer. I checked all the rooms and came upon a closed door. I opened the door. She was taking a bath.

Gracemary was the perfect wife. She was beautiful, intelligent, resourceful, a good homemaker, and she was pregnant. It was April 1972 and she was due in a couple of months. We now resided at Fort Devens. It was 10:00 pm, I was sleeping and there was a thunderstorm raging outside. Gracemary woke me and said that she wanted some calamari. I drove to the Boston Fish Market in Leominster, purchased an order, and drove home. Dripping wet, I handed her the calamari. She said she wasn't hungry.

June 23rd, 1972. Gracemary gave birth to our son, Matthew. I was in the delivery room with her. She insisted on natural childbirth and I still have the scar on my left hand from her fingernails.

Gracemary decided that since I was now a family man, a Mustang convertible was not the proper vehicle for a family's transportation. So I became my Dad, and forever more, I would be driving a sedan. It was great being a new Dad, but I wouldn't see my son blow out his first candle. The Army in its infinite wisdom decided to send me to Thailand. I left my family in Fitchburg, Massachusetts in April 1973.

Gracemary took care of the home front. In May 1973, she took Matthew to the pediatrician at the Fort Devens Cutler Army Hospital for a well baby check up. Matthew was a happy baby and always smiling. The pediatrician found an irregularity and another doctor came into the examination room. After several minutes of quite painful poking and prodding, the second doctor confirmed the first doctor's diagnosis. Then the hospital commander was summoned. After a brief consultation among all the doctors, the diagnosis was that Matthew had some rare baby condition (I don't remember the name, but it was a tongue twister) and if he didn't have immediate surgery, he would be dead in 24 hours.

Gracemary took her baby from the doctors and steadfastly walked out of the hospital. She put Matthew in his car carrier and drove 36 miles to the Boston Children's Hospital. She walked with a purpose through the entrance and approached a nurse. Holding back tears, she explained the events of the morning and wanted to see a doctor.

The nurse took Gracemary into an examination room and said, "Let me see your beautiful baby." She placed Matthew on an examination table, removed all his clothing, and gently started pressing around his abdomen. There was, what seemed to be, a large tumor present. The nurse kept gently massaging the lump on his abdomen and Matthew was gleefully cooing. Then she pressed with a little more pressure. Matthew was still cooing. More pressure and poof! Matthew's little body expelled baby poop.

After a doctor at Boston Children's Hospital gave Matthew a clean bill of health, Gracemary headed back to the Cutler Army Hospital. Holding on tightly to her baby, she walked with a purpose through the entrance. She walked to the nurses' station and demanded to see the hospital commander and the two idiots that hurt her baby that morning. An MP approached her; she glared at him and said, "Do not touch me!" The MP backed off. The colonel and two doctors arrived at the nurses' station. Gracemary then proceeded to read them all the riot act. She told them that this had been the worst day in the life of her happy baby; the two pediatricians were 'yes' men and didn't attempt to look beyond what seemed to be the obvious; if she had believed them, her baby would have undergone unnecessary and needless surgery; and this stupid incident could have traumatized her baby.

This single incident, in and of itself, was a significant emotional event that caused Gracemary to develop a healthy pessimism and general distrust of the Military establishment and to never accept command edicts at face value. In the course of the next twenty-plus years, Gracemary's doubts were proven correct more often than not.

DOMINIC JAMES INGEMI

Dominic J. Ingemi was a U.S. Navy Chief Petty Officer and combat veteran of World War II. At nearly six feet tall and 260 pounds, he was a mountain of a man in physical appearance, stature and spirit. He was one of the greatest men I have ever known. The first time I ever met him was in December of 1970. The occasion was to take his daughter out to dinner. He invited me into his kitchen, told me to have a seat and set before me a plate on which was a giant mushroom that he had personally picked and prepared with his own special sauce. I consumed the feast before me much to the chagrin of his daughter.

Dominic Ingemi was a loving family man and successful businessman. He had five children; two daughters and three sons. His eldest daughter, Gracemary, became my wife on May 1st, 1971. He built and owned the Mohawk Club, a family restaurant and dinner club that eventually evolved into a popular night club that headlined 1960's up and coming music entertainers and bands. He sold the club and opened a quiet little neighborhood bar and grille located near an amusement park. His new business was successful and he sold it to go into an early retirement. Then, as a past time, he would sit at his kitchen table and read the newspaper searching for businesses in which to invest. Dominic James Ingemi found his niche as an entrepreneur.

Dominic was the family patriarch and my third son was named after him. His favorite past time was cooking. He enjoyed family gatherings, entertaining his grandchildren and cooking family meals. On an early summer late afternoon in 1985, he was preparing dinner for his family when he suffered a heart attack and died at his kitchen table. He was doing what he enjoyed most as he quietly departed this world.

Circa early 1970s. A professor from a small community college in south west Texas developed a theory based on his own family experience. He named his theory "The Abilene Paradox." He made a film for the U.S. Army and in it he presented a lecture on his theory. The film, 8 mm, was distributed throughout the Army and became a part of mandatory training. Of all the mandatory training I was ever required to attend, this subject made the greatest impression on me and I applied the professor's principles to nearly every aspect of my adult life. It is simplicity in itself. When confronted with a situation that just seems downright dumb, more likely than not, it is. So don't be afraid to ask questions. Sometimes, and history repeats itself more often than not, people do things because it's what they think their leaders want. When in actuality, the end result isn't even remotely close to what was the original intent of the leader.

The professor's family lived on a farm in the remote countryside of south west Texas. It was an unbearably hot and dusty Texas in July day. The young children were gleefully playing in the front yard, the adults were sweltering in the kitchen trying to get whatever breeze they could from a single electric fan, and Grandpa was sitting in his rocker on the front porch just rocking back and forth and back and forth. Grandpa was silently watching the children play as he was rocking in his chair. Then, he made a comment to himself that was overheard by one of the adults. Grandpa said, "It sure would be nice to go to Abilene." Then the adults said to each other, "Grandpa wants to go to Abilene." So the whole family was packed into the family station wagon and they were off to Abilene. There was no air conditioning, so the windows were rolled down and the dusty air circulated throughout the car. It was an uncomfortable, bumpy, hot dusty trip. And all the while, Grandpa was sitting in the back of the station wagon saying to himself, "Why the hell are we going to Abilene?"

There were numerous occasions I related the Abilene story to people who worked for me. Throughout my career, I tried not to send people on a bus to Abilene, and insisted on clear instructions when given a task that really didn't make a whole lot of sense. Sometimes instructions were clarified and other times they weren't. Then it was a crapshoot. I was hoping I put in motion the right thing to do. Other times there was a comedy of errors and I'd be walking down the hallway saying out loud, "We have our tickets and we're on the bus to Abilene." People knew what I was talking about.

THE BOXER AND THE BLACK BELT

Circa 1971. My roommate when I attended the 1ˢᵗ Army Noncommissioned Officer Academy at Fort Dix, New Jersey was Staff Sergeant Darryl W. Coots. He progressed in his Military career to become an Airborne Division Command Sergeant Major. Darryl was the Heavyweight Boxing Champion, VII Corps, U.S. Army Europe and his wife held a black belt in one of the martial arts. Personally, I wouldn't want to meet Darryl's wife in a dark alley.

Being roommates, we exchanged war stories. My most harrowing experience was TET '68 with operations in the Tumerong Valley bringing in a close second. Darryl was in the Ashau Valley with the 101ˢᵗ Airborne Division at the same time my brother, Mike was there. Darryl was severely wounded and medevac'd to a field hospital. Triage was set up for all the wounded soldiers being shuttled in and when the medics got to Darryl, one of them said, "Leave him, he's a goner."

Darryl had assignment orders to the Academy as an Instructor. But before he could perform his duties, he had to attend the Academy as a student. A cardinal rule when attending a Military school that may cause the student mental or physical anguish and duress is to keep a low profile and never give an Instructor cause to remember your name. Darryl was screwed. And, by proxy, me too. Our first room inspection we accumulated 50 demerits. It's virtually impossible to get 50 demerits during the whole four weeks of attending the Academy.

Curriculum was Basic Military Leadership, Drill and Ceremonies, Land Navigation, Leading Physical Fitness Training and prior to graduation, an Army Physical Fitness Test. The first three weeks was attending training and working off demerits. We only accumulated 10 demerits after the first disastrous inspection. Which, by the way, the instructors joked about after we graduated.

Our graduation ceremony was in the morning and that evening the Instructors had a party welcoming Darryl to the NCO Academy. He invited me since, not by choice but for survival, we had become friends. There was a buffet and punch bowl and other beverages. It was a good time. The Instructors' wives were present, as well as Darryl's wife. Darryl and I were talking to a couple of Instructors when his wife came over and suggested that they leave. Darryl had an empty glass in his hand and said he would get another drink and then they would be on their way. Standing in front of us, she kicked the glass, it glided toward her, and she caught it. She said, "That's OK honey, I'll get it for you."

In April 1973, I was assigned to Thailand in the mountains near the Laotian border. Thailand is a beautiful country and for anyone else it was paradise. But for me, it was to be a year of not being in Special Forces and an assignment in purgatory. No Viet Nam buddies, no jumping out of airplanes and no running around the woods. At least Thailand had a jungle. My new unit was the 7th Radio Research Field Station, a United States Army Security Agency strategic electronic intelligence collection facility.

I never thought much of my Military rank; I was a Staff Sergeant. I had five years in grade and was the ranking Staff Sergeant on the facility. What it meant in Special Forces was that on a grass cutting detail, I had a push mower. A Senior Noncommissioned Officer had a power lawnmower. In Special Forces, we all worked together, regardless of rank, to accomplish the mission. In the Regular Army, a Staff Sergeant stood around and gave orders while other people did the work. That wasn't me. I worked side by side with my people, we got the job done in half the time, and I didn't believe in "make work." When they finished whatever had to be done, the rest of the day was theirs. I did the "spook" stuff for six months and was starting to like it. That's when I first started working counterdrug and was in charge of the intelligence collection mission targeted against drug runners in the Golden Triangle.

In November 1973, I interviewed for the Senior Enlisted position in the Aviation Section. I was selected over other Aviation Noncommissioned Officers who had air combat experience in Viet Nam. So now I was the Noncommissioned Officer-in-Charge (NCOIC). My call sign was "Snoopy 58." I flew in RU-21D Communications Intelligence turbo prop planes and others in my section flew in RU-21J Electronic Intelligence turbo prop planes. It was a fun six months and I really enjoyed flying.

All my missions were air combat hours; we didn't fly missions in Thailand. Our targets were Pathe Lao and North Vietnamese Army. We had one mission that lasted two weeks that was strictly voluntary. I took the D-bird and one of my NCOs took the J-bird. We were tasked by the National Security Agency (NSA) to locate Chinese Communist

(CHICOM) anti-aircraft batteries (SAM sites) located adjacent to a road being built by the Chinese that ran from the northern Laotian border to the southern border at Thailand. We called the road "the yellow brick road." My aircraft flew the road and the other aircraft flew off our wing about one mile. We were taunting the Chinese to go into a firing sequence. Once they had a lock, a radical change of direction would break the lock. This game of cat and mouse went on for two weeks and we located all the SAM missile sites on the road.

I completed my assignment in Thailand and received orders for my next assignment to Okinawa. I was going back to Special Forces. I was being assigned to the 400th Special Operations Detachment (Airborne), 1st Special Forces Group (Airborne), 1st Special Forces located at Camp Chinen, Okinawa.

THE SUPER JOCK

Circa 1973, Camp Chinen, Okinawa: Headquarters, 1st Special Forces Group (Airborne) and subordinate units including 400th Special Operations Detachment (Airborne).

I was assigned to the 400th SOD in May 1973 after spending a year at the United States Army Security Agency 7th Radio Research Field Station located at Udorn, Thailand. I survived my year of purgatory outside Special Forces imposed upon me by Department of the Army and was reunited with some of my friends from the 402nd and 403rd SOD's. We were a tight-knit group of young men and welcomed newcomers as equals. It is difficult to explain, but there is a bond among those who have served in combat together. It's something that others don't share. We also were the best at what we did and didn't have to prove it to anyone. It was just a fact. And, once a year, we had to play Army. All your accomplishments including combat experience, parachuting, land navigation, mountain climbing, water survival, escape and evasion, languages and a multitude of other talents didn't mean squat unless you took the annual APFT (Army Physical Fitness Test). The APFT consisted of a minimum to maximum number of correct pushups and sit-ups and a timed two-mile run. That was it. Each APFT event had a minimum score of 60 and a maximum score of 100. A max score for the APFT was 300. Not impossible, but attainable. During my career, I max'd the test twice; once in 1974 and the next to last test I took before retirement in 1994, just to do it. My final test, I achieved a perfect minimum score and took everyone out for coffee afterward.

The 1973 APFT was coming up. We were assigned a new supply sergeant. He came to us from outside Special Forces and wasn't "S" qualified. But that was OK because he didn't need to be. He was, however, airborne qualified. And, an over-achiever. He excelled at everything he tried and was quite vocal about it. For two weeks before the test, he talked about how he was going to max it. We sort of encouraged him whenever he started talking about what he would do. The big day arrived.

The Sergeant Major held formation at 0600 (6:00 am). All forty-four personnel were present and accounted for. A previously selected core of graders had taken the test and would be administering the APFT to the remainder of the unit. The pushup and sit-up portions were administered. We all did minimum requirements and the supply sergeant attained the maximum score in each event. There was a short break and then time for the two-mile run. The route was pre-measured on relatively flat terrain at Camp Chinen considering we were on top of a mountain. The run started and ended at our unit headquarters building. ICHI—NICHI—GO!

The Sergeant Major held his accountability formation at 0900 (9:00 am). He congratulated everyone on passing the annual Army Physical Fitness Test and called the supply sergeant front and center. The Sergeant Major praised the supply sergeant for his perfect score of 300 on the test. The Sergeant Major's wife, the supply sergeant's wife and other unit member's wives then exited the Orderly Room and approached the two men in front of the formation. The Sergeant Major's wife handed her husband a large wooden plaque.

The Sergeant Major called the formation to Attention. He then gave a dissertation about the importance of physical fitness and formally presented the plaque to the supply sergeant. The plaque had been designed by the unit wives, to include the supply sergeant's wife. It was to be presented to the one person who excelled at the APFT. Rules were, if more than one person excelled, the Sergeant Major would select the recipient. However, there was only one person.

The plaque itself was 10x14 cherrywood. One half of the plaque was inscribed with the 400th SOD unit designation, a narrative and a map of Okinawa. The other half had a lace-trimmed athletic supporter mounted upon it.

OKINAWA RETURNED TO JAPAN

Circa Spring 1974. I was at Taegu, Korea with my team. We had completed a crash Korean language course at Camp Chinen, Okinawa in February 1974 and then deployed on a training exercise to Korea with advance elements of the 1st Special Forces Group. The training exercise lasted 30 days.

After returning to Okinawa from Korea, we had to pack equipment and prepare it for shipment to the United States. Under the terms of an agreement with the Japanese government regarding the return of Okinawa to Japan, designated U.S. Military combat units would leave Japanese soil. The 1st Special Forces Group was one of those units; returned to Fort Bragg, North Carolina; and was officially deactivated on June 30th, 1974.

The 400th Special Operations Detachment was spared being inactivated because the 5th Special Forces Group had been brought back to life and didn't have a Special Operations Detachment. So in June 1974, the John F. Kennedy Center For Military Assistance assigned the 400th SOD to the 5th Special Forces Group.

The 1ˢᵗ Special Forces Group was gone. The 400ᵗʰ SOD was assigned to the 5ᵗʰ Special Forces Group which had an area of operations oriented toward the Middle East. There weren't many senior-level combat-experienced people assigned to the Group. There wasn't anyone from the 1ˢᵗ Group to advocate for us. We were somewhat placed in a position of having to prove ourselves.

In the mean time, we ended up on ash and trash details. At least, that's what it seemed like. I was a Staff Sergeant, so I got a push mower and didn't have to use a sling blade. My best friend Bob was a Master Sergeant, so he had a mower with a motor. I'm being facetious, but we did perform a lot of details for the Group S3 (Operations). We did everything we were tasked to do. And we did it better than anyone else. Bob and a couple other Senior NCOs worked behind the scenes to get us out of the predicament we were in. In the mean time, we had a motto: "We don't do windows." One of the jokesters in the unit even made a placard with our motto and hung it under our unit sign in front of the orderly room.

Then it happened: We received a tasking from the Group S3 to clean windows at the John F. Kennedy Center for Military Assistance. That whole complex is double-pane glass windows.

The Group S3 was a jokester himself. He saw the sign and sent us the tasking. Officially, the ash and trash period was over and we were ending 1974 with school allocations and real world mission assignments supporting the 5ᵗʰ Special Forces Group.

1975 was a good year. Senior people were being assigned to the 5ᵗʰ Special Forces Group who had served with my friends and me in Vietnam. So there was nothing to prove to them. Also, my buddy Joe came to Fort Bragg. There is a story about Joe later on. Joe was a catalyst for my career taking off like a rocket.

1975 was the year I was selected ahead of my peers out of the secondary zone for promotion to Sergeant First Class. My career progression saw two more future promotions from the secondary zone…First Sergeant and Sergeant Major.

Escape and Evasion (E&E)

Circa 1975. The training mission was to parachute into Uhwarrie National Forest, link up with a guerilla band, and disrupt enemy ground force operations in the area. The enemy in this case was elements of the 82nd Airborne Division. My job would be to provide force protection to the Special Forces team I was accompanying by keeping electronic tabs on the 82nd.

The plane arrived over the drop zone at 2:00 am, received the go-ahead signal from the ground, and we were given the green light to go. I was in the middle of a 13-man stick and just before reaching the door, my equipment got caught on a collapsible aircraft seat. The remainder of the stick went past me and out the door. I ripped the seat, including aluminum frame, out of the fuselage and headed toward the door. As I reached the door, the light turned red to abort and the Air Force cargo master placed his arm in front of me to block my exit. I pushed him out of my way and jumped into the darkness holding on to the aircraft seat that was still entangled in my equipment.

I wasn't over the drop zone, but I could see activity on the ground. The drop zone was surrounded and illuminated by vehicle lights of 82nd Airborne Division vehicles. The team was captured as each person landed. I steered my parachute toward the edge of the drop zone behind the enemy forces. I landed on railroad tracks and there was a train coming in the distance. I collected my parachute and secured it at the edge of the drop zone. Then I circled the drop zone and headed toward the prisoner containment area. I could see that everyone was alright, procured a communications codebook and frequencies from a jeep, and departed the area.

I was officially entering the Escape and Evasion (E&E) network. Once I was far enough away and found a safe area, I encrypted a message about the team's status, included intelligence I had collected, cut an antenna and transmitted via Morse code to the Special Forces Operations Base (SFOB) at Fort Bragg using my PRC-92 battery-powered transmitter. My communications equipment was a CIA experimental AM transmitter/receiver about the size of a carton of cigarettes including the battery pack and weighed about two pounds. My message was acknowledged and I took off.

I made contact with the owner of a small country store and worked in his store stocking shelves for about five days. Exercise controllers and soldiers from the 82nd shopped at the store and asked us to call them if a soldier who was lost came into the store. We said that we would.

The 82nd ran their prisoner compound and the team sat and waited. When I received an all clear message from Fort Bragg, I got back into uniform and linked up with the team after they were released. We then continued with the training mission.

Women in the Military were confined to clerical, intelligence or medical noncombatant jobs until the mid-1970s. Then Women's Rights happened. They could do the same job as a male; just as good if not better. It was a man's Army and typical thinking in the trenches was, "Yeah, Right!" I say this only because of the first time I met Kathy. The United States Army had the audacity to assign a female buck sergeant to Special Forces, and my unit no less! I was Staff Duty NCO the night our new radio-teletype operator showed up fresh out of jump school (female paratrooper?) and duffel bag over her shoulder.

Sergeant Kathy Picon was a super-soldier. Our daily training was physically demanding and she was there with or in front of us all the way. No quarter asked, none given. Whether it was the Bear Pit (martial arts, knife fighting, hand-to-hand), rappelling, water survival, running or a myriad of other tasks, she was right there. Kathy became a Master Parachutist and Jump Master and was responsible for the lives of the paratroopers on her manifest. After I left the unit in 1981, I lost touch with her. The last I heard when I retired in 1995 was that she was a Master Sergeant and on the promotion list to Sergeant Major.

Captain Katie Elder was a Military Intelligence officer who was a member of the Military Intelligence unit that was incorporated into mine circa 1980. Katie was a "spook". She was also another super-soldier and a friend for many years at Fort Bragg. Katie fought with the Department of the Army for many years to attend the Special Forces Qualification Course. She also had political and pentagon backing, but Special Forces is combat-arms and it didn't happen...until. I think it was around 1977 or 1978 when she received approval with a caveat. She could attend, but if by some snowball's chance in hell she should complete training and graduate, she wouldn't be assigned to a Special Forces A-Team and she wouldn't be allowed to wear the Green Beret. Long, grueling story short, Katie graduated. I proudly attended her graduation ceremony. Some of my peers couldn't accept it. They were dinosaurs on the verge of a new Army horizon. Women were here to stay. No quarter asked...none given.

Joe was a character. Nickname: Pirate. We first met in Viet Nam. Joe had this stupid little toy parrot he would place on his shoulder and he would go into a pirate routine with a deep, raspy pirate voice. It was hilarious. Joe's voice barking out pirate-type orders could be heard over the sound of explosions in the background and M-16's and AK-47's firing.

After Viet Nam, Joe was assigned to one of the Airborne Divisions, 82nd or 101st. During a training parachuting operation, he shattered an ankle and was medically retired. Sergeant First Class Joseph Langevin was recruited by the Defense Intelligence Agency (DIA) and was Chief, Special Projects Division. Joe travelled from Washington to Fort Bragg and briefed the Commander and the G2 (Intelligence Officer) on a project in development to support Special Operations Forces in wartime. He requested that I be his point of contact at Fort Bragg. So, I had a new additional duty. I was the United States Army John F. Kennedy Center for Military Assistance representative to the Defense Intelligence Agency for Special Operations Projects.

PROJECT TRACER ROUND I and PROJECT TRACER ROUND III covered a three year period from 1975 to 1978. As phases were implemented, I would either go to Washington or Joe would come to Fort Bragg. Joe had a noticeable limp from his training accident and he exaggerated the limp when he visited my home. My two young boys loved him and he had my family in stitches with his pirate routine. Joe could stay in character for hours. The only part of the project I'll mention is that it involved detecting, locating and neutralizing certain warhead-tipped SCUD missiles on the ground. I also tested the prototype for the 50-caliber sniper rifle which played an important part in the success of the project.

In late 1977, when we were almost finished with the project's final phase, I asked Joe about TRACER ROUND II. He told me there wasn't one. U.S. Counter Intelligence had discovered that foreign intelligence agencies were attempting to collect information on the TRACER ROUND projects. So, after TRACER ROUND I was completed, he put together TRACER ROUND III to frustrate foreign intelligence collection efforts. Joe's ruse was successful.

Joe was an avid camper. In late 1978, he was by himself on a camping trip in the Everglades and was killed in a camping accident. However, safety was always foremost with him and he was an expert camper. Cause of death: Accidental. My speculation: Something that Americans believe never happens on U.S. soil.

Circa 1976. Late summer. This story was reported in detail in a full-page newspaper article in the Fayetteville Observer, Fayetteville, North Carolina. Rather than rely wholly on my memory, I attempted to look at on-line archives, but they only went back to 1988. So here's the story as I remember the way it happened. It was a warm, sunny day and I had gone home for lunch around noon. When I entered the front door, Gracemary, my wife, was on the phone in the dining room sitting at the dining room table. She had a very concerned and determined look on her face. Speaking in a calm, forceful voice, she was telling the person on the other end of the line to be calm and describe his surroundings. I walked over to the table and she wrote me a note, "SUICIDE."

Gracemary wrote me another note to call the police. I went to four or five neighbors' houses and nobody was at home. This was before 911, call-waiting and cell phones. Telephones were still attached to cords and you couldn't move six feet in any given direction. I finally found a neighbor at home and asked to use the phone. I called the police, and since my house was in Cumberland County and not Fayetteville, I was transferred to the Sheriff's Department. About a half hour later, a deputy arrived at my house.

Gracemary had been on the phone a half hour before I got home and then another half hour passed. She had a stack of notes in front of her and all the while she was listening and talking with Raymond. The deputy called his dispatch and requested a court order to trace the phone call. Gracemary kept up her conversation. She asked Raymond what he could see through the window. He said that he could see the back of the Observer. The deputy contacted the Fayetteville police and a while later they reported back to him that there weren't any buildings behind the Fayetteville Observer.

Two hours passed since Gracemary answered the phone and Raymond was on the other end. The Sheriff's Department had the court order and the phone company complied. However, it was 1970's mechanical technology and a long way from today's satellite triangulation. Quadrants had to be checked and cleared. Another hour went by. Three hours on the phone. Gracemary's voice was hoarse and she was telling Raymond to stay on the line with her. He said he had to go.

Gracemary yelled into the phone, "No Raymond!" There was commotion and a lot of noise on the other end of the line. Then silence. Gracemary said, "Raymond?" More silence. Then, a voice on the other end said, "Mrs. Carden?" She answered, "Yes" and the voice on the other end said that they had Raymond in protective custody.

When Raymond said he could see the back of the Observer, he was telling the truth. The Fayetteville Observer had recently moved into a new building and Raymond was looking through the window of his apartment at the back of the old building.

SPECIAL TERRAIN PARACHUTING TECHNIQUES

I am one of a hand full of people who successfully completed a special course of parachuting into rough terrain that consisted mainly of forests and rocky mountainous areas. We wore special padded protective clothing to protect vital organs and protective headgear that resembled a football helmet with a mesh screen over the face. Additional equipment included a K-Bar survival knife for cutting parachute suspension lines and harness webbing, a hand-made Swiss-seat with snap link for rappelling, and stowed in the right leg cargo pocket was 150 feet of nylon rappelling rope. The idea was to successfully parachute into unreachable areas with minimal injuries and continue with the mission.

We had ten day and ten night parachute jumps over the forested areas of Fort Bragg, North Carolina. The idea was if caught in trees you could rappel down to the ground. Personally, I had no intention of hanging upside down 60 feet in the air, tying off my rappelling rope on the parachute harness, and rappelling down to the ground. But that's what I did. I had the pleasure of utilizing this skill in the mountains of South Korea. However, nobody told us that Korean mountains, besides having tall trees, also have boulders the size of a house. That was my experience utilizing Special Terrain Parachuting Techniques. One skill I don't mind not using any more.

Used To Be

There was a grouping of soldiers who were in the Army from the mid-1950s to the mid-1970s whom I call the "used to be" soldiers. They dwelled in the past. I knew some of them. Most were in conventional units and I met a few in Special Forces. They were the constant complainers who never offered any solutions on how to make things better. I once heard a comment that "a happy soldier is a bitching soldier." These guys must have been extremely happy.

They reminisced and praised how great things were in the "Old Army." They never provided examples of how great things were; they just didn't like how things were at the time they were in. It's true that times weren't really great for the Military Services during the late 1960s and early 1970s. The primary reason was that our country was going through a huge sociological upheaval. But, for the American Soldier, it was really better than prior to World War II. Pay was better and opportunities for education and promotions were better.

Soldiers could get their GED or a college degree through on-campus study, night school, or by correspondence. Plus, military education was available by taking any of hundreds of correspondence courses. Education, both civilian and military, contributed toward promotion points for younger soldiers. NCOs and soldiers on the promotion list could attend the Primary Leadership Development Course (PLDC) or the NCO Academy. Mid-level NCOs could attend the Basic Noncommissioned Officer Course (BNOC) and Senior NCOs could attend the Advanced Noncommissioned Officer Course (ANCOC). The Army was grooming educated leaders. Education was one of the qualifiers for promotion. The Army was looking for a balance of diversified assignments, education and leadership.

The "used to be" soldiers couldn't or wouldn't adapt to change and they went the way of the dinosaur. They were retired before things really started getting bad. They were gone before the Carter years.

Circa 1977 to 1981. There are more learned people than me that can write about Jimmy Carter's presidency. I can only say that from day one, the Military started belt tightening; there was a 444 day black mark painted on the United States of America; eight American Servicemen died attempting to wipe away that black mark; and one payback is still owed.

The Military operated on a shoestring budget and the politicians were in essence dismantling our Armed Forces. Tough times for career soldiers. We were fast approaching the Army of pre-World War II. Entrance standards were lowered and Category Four people were accepted for first term enlistments. The Services, which primarily meant the Army, were forced to accept non-high school graduates and it took ten years to correct the situation for those soldiers who hadn't attained a high school GED while on active duty.

Young soldiers with families didn't make enough money to support their loved ones and some were actually on welfare rolls. Nobody cared outside the Military what was happening to them and this most of all, in my opinion, was a National Disgrace.

Although soldiers were struggling to make ends meet, politicians in congress ensured their pay increases were in order. That has a familiar ring today.

Special Forces and Military Intelligence weren't hit as hard as the rest of the Army, but we still felt the crunch. Operational, maintenance and training budgets were tight. I was a Team Sergeant. There were many times that I, as well as other leaders, spent my own money just to buy basic cleaning supplies because there was no money in the budget. It seems that all Team Sergeants were Radio Shack's best customers because we bought communications equipment repair parts from them. Once, I was detained for a short while by the Military Police because I was inside an exchange shoppette during morning "prime training time." I had just purchased a box of steel wool pads to clean FM radio antennas and my Team Room was located down an embankment about 90 feet from the back door. Times were getting stupid.

If we had a training mission away from Fort Bragg, and had to fly on Air Force aircraft, we had to pay the Air Force for the transportation.

But, if we flew on an Air Force aircraft and parachuted into our destination, we didn't have to pay the Air Force because we weren't inside the aircraft when it landed. The pilots were getting "flying time" under their belts.

I have one final thing to say about the Carter years. The best thing that happened for the Military Services and America during the Carter administration was that Ronald Reagan was elected the next President of the United States.

PARACHUTE LANDING FALL

A parachute landing fall (PLF) is the ability to successfully crash into the ground at a high rate of speed without being seriously injured after exiting a perfectly good aircraft from an extremely high altitude.

Circa July 1978. 5th Special Forces Group Organization Day. This event is an annual picnic and day of fun and activities for Group members and their families that includes a tug-of-war, foot races, alligator petting, a miniature jump tower for children, and a myriad of other fun activities. Also included are a HALO demonstration (High Altitude, Low Opening) and an all day helicopter parachuting event.

Adjacent to the drop zone was an asphalt parking area (hardstand in Military terminology) that several family members, including my own, stood on to observe the parachuting demonstrations.

As I was leaving my wife and six-year-old son, Matthew, to draw my parachute and reserve, my son asked me a question. He said, "Daddy, I know what you say when you jump out of an airplane, but what do you say when you land on the ground?" I said, Matthew, I usually say UNNNGGGGHHHH!" He thanked me for this enlightenment as I was headed toward the loading area.

I was Jumpmaster for this, the first of three or four jumps for me that day, and I was the last to exit the helicopter. I put five jumpers out and followed the last one. Jumper number four had blown panels and his reserve was partially deployed. He was in dire straights and at the mercy of the wind as he was being carried directly toward the hardstand. I steered my chute toward him and followed him in. I could see him preparing for what was surely to be an extremely painful encounter with asphalt.

The ambulance was on its way. From my vantage point above him, I saw him execute the most perfect Parachute Landing Fall ever accomplished by a paratrooper. He simultaneously landed on the balls of his feet, tucked his elbows into his ribcage gripping his front risers in front of his face as he twisted to the side, impacting the fleshy part of his buttocks and rolling onto the pushup muscle on the back of his shoulder as his forward momentum propelled him across several feet of asphalt.

This happened about twenty feet from my wife and son. When he landed, the jumper let out a loud "UNNNGGGGHHHH!" Matthew excitedly said to his Mother, "Mommy, Mommy, he did it right!"

The jumper recovered his parachute and turned it in to the Riggers for examination. He then drew another chute for his next jump.

Circa 1978. I don't remember the exact time, but it was just before the Shah fell. I had the opportunity to meet Shah Pahlavi and his lovely wife. My mission was to support intelligence requirements by keeping tabs on something the Soviets were doing. My cover was performing duty as the radio operator with a Special Forces A-Team from the 3rd Battalion, 5th Special Forces Group. The white mission was to train the Shah's Imperial Guard who were Iranian Special Forces, test border police at the Pakistan border, drug interdiction (hashish) coming out of Pakistan, and train the Baluchi tribesmen in mountain warfare. The Iranian radio operator hurt his hand when we parachuted into Baluchistan in southern Iran, so I took care of his Morse contacts with Tehran. This involved sending and receiving Morse code special text using their encryption system. Their Morse communications were being jammed and I was able to determine who the culprits were and overcame that nuisance. The time spent with Iranian encryption systems came in handy later when the government changed hands.

Training the Baluchi's went quite well. A few years later, I read in a newspaper articled that it took the Revolutionary Guard two years to track them all down.

When we were in the desert, a special envoy and Iranian government official flew out by helicopter to see us. They brought a package with them. We had been provided blood chits when we were in Tehran. A blood chit is basically a silk scarf with a message written in the language of whatever country you're visiting. In this case, the language was both Farsi and Arabic. The blood chits requested assistance and whoever helped us would be rewarded. That's what we thought they said. The blood chits were taken away from us and we were provided new chits. It seems the literal translation of the original blood chits was: "Return my body to the Imperial Palace and you will be rewarded." There wasn't any wiggle room or room for negotiation. The Iranian government was really embarrassed by this little faux pas.

Testing the border police went well except for one little glitch. Tehran didn't tell them we would be there. When we attacked at 2:00 am with blank ammunition and pyrotechnics, they shot at us with live ammunition. Everything was smoothed over with coffee and pastries.

We interdicted one hashish caravan and reported their location to Tehran. Our meeting was uneventful. Although we were outnumbered, they had Soviet MATS-36 bolt-action rifles and we were armed to the teeth with CAR-15 automatic weapons and grenades if needed.

When working with foreign Armies, there are certain protocols that take place. One thing is exchanging uniform items. Patches, hats, boots, whatever. It's camaraderie. The next thing is formal. When it comes to paratroopers, jumping together is considered a joint international operation and participants are awarded the parachutist badge of the respective country. They receive our parachutist badge and we receive theirs. I have the Vietnamese Parachutist Badge for jumping in the Mekong Delta; and the Royal Imperial Iranian Parachutist Badge for jumping into Baluchistan. When I retired, I was the last soldier on active duty to possess the Iranian Parachutist Badge.

THE CUTE LITTLE LAMB

Circa 1978. It was late morning and the sun was beating down on the cement-hard, cracked gray desert floor. The temperature was over 110 degrees and we were resting at an oasis outside a village in the Province of Baluchistan in southern Iran. Water at the oasis wasn't potable because it was alkaline. We had enough water to last us a couple of days until we reached the next oasis.

I was sitting under a bush without leaves trying to gain some semblance of shade while I was encrypting a message to send to Tehran by Morse code. I heard a lamb baa'ing from behind me as I was writing my message. Then two Baluchi tribesmen came around the bush from behind with a little black and white lamb in tow. They brought the lamb to me and I was looking into its big brown eyes as I was petting it. The tribesmen were smiling and laughing as I was petting the cute little lamb and I thanked them in Arabic for bringing it to me. I also told them that Americans appreciate little animals, especially the very young.

The Baluchi tribesmen had gone into the village earlier and purchased the little lamb and brought it back to our camp. I was petting the lamb and they told me that they had to go. I bid them farewell and went back to encrypting my message. They led the little lamb away and I could hear it baa'ing as they crossed the camp…baa, baa, baa.

I could still hear the lamb baa'ing when it changed to Glaa! Glaa! The cute little lamb was their lunch.

Circa 1978. We returned from Iran. Our plane landed at 2:00 am at Pope Air Force Base next to Fort Bragg, North Carolina. The plane taxied to a tarmac in the middle of nowhere. An Air Force vehicle picked up the plane crew and left. Naturally, no one had come to meet us.

The only thing to do was to mount up, grab your equipment, and walk home. There were lights in the distance that beckoned us. A bunch of guys dressed in black, beards caked in desert dust, carrying rucksacks and rifles started walking across the runway at a huge Air Force Base. We walked for a few minutes and were surrounded by Air Police with vehicle-mounted machine guns and dogs. We were detained and the 5th Special Forces Group Staff Duty Officer had to drive to Pope and sign for us. After securing our weapons and equipment, we each went to our respective homes about 4:00 am. I didn't have my house key, so I broke out my sleeping bag and sacked out under a tree in the back yard. I was awakened by Matthew and Steven, my two young sons, who were having the time of their lives spraying me with a garden hose. I needed the shower anyway. It took a few days for the arrest incident to die down. We thought it was funny, but the Air Force didn't have a sense of humor.

The 5th Special Forces Group was preparing for a huge training exercise at Hurlburt Field, Eglin Air Force Base, Florida. We spent about a week preparing and packing our equipment in shipment boxes. Then it was secured in conex containers for the flight to Florida on cargo planes. Vehicles would make the trip by convoy. Somebody had to be the Convoy Commander. Among the three Team Sergeants, a decision had to be made. Someone had to step up to the plate and take charge. Since nobody volunteered, we decided to draw names from a hat. I felt pretty comfortable with that idea because I never win anything.

I was looking forward to the next two days riding about 750 miles in a Military three-quarter ton truck that had canvas covered seats as comfortable as a cinder block. Forty-five to fifty miles-per-hour heading due south on I-95. A fun ride lay ahead.

Circa 1978. Driving 750 miles in a Military three-quarter ton truck builds character. It also creates aches and pains in places you never knew you had. The fun was over and it was time to get down to business.

I was in charge of creating the first 5th Special Forces Group All Source Production Center (ASPC). The facility that I established was the predecessor to the Sensitive Compartmented Information Facilities (SCIF) that are in use today by intelligence agencies and all the Military Services. The ASPC was up and running for the training exercise and could also handle real-time real-world intelligence if required.

There wasn't a lot going on, so I took an AN/PRC-92 AM radio transmitter-receiver, some antenna wire, and a Morse-code leg key and went into the woods. I was going to find a ham radio operator and practice sending and receiving Morse code.

As I was searching the frequency spectrum for a ham radio operator, I came across something that I recognized and shouldn't be hearing in the Western Hemisphere. I built a make-shift hand-held radio direction finding antenna, attained a null on the signal which was very strong, and took an azimuth with my lensatic compass. The signal obviously wasn't coming from the north, so I had a very reliable azimuth that headed due south. The next land mass was Cuba.

I returned to the ASPC and sent a message back to Fort Bragg with information for appropriate distribution.

National news agencies, at a later date, reported that there were two Soviet Army Engineer Battalions in Cuba.

REDTRAIN

Circa July 1979 to July 1981. In the summer of 1979, Military Intelligence units were being transitioned from strategic intelligence collection to tactical intelligence collection. Military Intelligence soldiers were being assigned to tactical units in the combat divisions. This was something new. So, whoever was in charge of the alphabet soup for unit designations at Department of the Army had to come up with titles for these new combat tactical intelligence units. Why not call them Combat Tactical Intelligence companies and battalions? Short designators would be CBTI Company and CBTI Battalion. The whole alphabet soup thing really didn't make any sense, so stand-alone CBTIs went the way of the dodo bird in a matter of a few months. But there was a general or politician somewhere who liked the term CBTI, so Military Intelligence units were redesignated as MI Company (CBTI) and MI Battalion (CBTI). Eventually, (CBTI) just went away. Maybe whoever was involved with its inception had retired.

Since Military Intelligence soldiers assigned to tactical units couldn't maintain their strategic intelligence collection skills, a budgeted program was developed at Department of the Army to allow soldiers to travel to strategic locations to work for short periods and maintain their skills. There were some smart people in the Office of the Deputy Chief of Staff for Intelligence (DCSI) at Department of the Army. They figured out how to get money out of the Army and not have to use operational or training funds to get live intelligence training for soldiers in tactical units. They called it Live Environment Training (LET) and the Intelligence Readiness Training Program (REDTRAIN) was born. Every tactical intelligence unit in the Army would receive REDTRAIN funds. Special Forces was no exception. I'll get this out of the way now. While the Army was playing with alphabet soup, the 400th Special Operations Detachment became a "CBTI (Special Forces)" and a few months later, it became the 14th MI Company, 5th Special Forces Group, followed by just MI Company, 5th Special Forces Group. Regardless of what the Army was doing, we were still the 400th Special Operations Detachment.

The summer of 1979 was a turning point in my career. I reluctantly gave up my Team and moved up to take over Operations (S-3) for the 400th SOD/CBTI (SF)/14th MI Co/MI Co, 5th SFG. Initially, my primary responsibilities were to plan and coordinate world-wide unit personnel deployments for on-the-ground operations and training in support of the 5th Special Forces Group. The advent of REDTRAIN opened a whole new realm of training opportunities for my fellow soldiers. I was now responsible for getting them quality intelligence training on a shoestring budget. I was appointed as my unit REDTRAIN NCO and as our higher headquarters REDTRAIN Officer. So now I worked directly for my immediate Commander and the Commander, 5th Special Forces Group.

The first order of business was to find out what REDTRAIN was all about. Nobody really knew. I went to the Pentagon to find out. What I found out was amazing and I also acquired points of contact at the Pentagon for future endeavors. What I discovered, which was really no secret but nobody had asked, was that the office for the whole United States Army REDTRAIN Program was manned and controlled by two people...a Captain and a Sergeant First Class. They were given the job and told to "make it happen." They also had control of $10,000,000.00 to disburse to Major Commands (MACOM) in the United States and around the world. They were genuinely glad that I had arrived, because all they were getting were electronic messages from units around the world demanding money for tactical intelligence training. It was a great learning experience for me. They explained how the program was supposed to work and what training benefits soldiers would receive. They provided me with a draft copy of the Army regulation governing REDTRAIN and told me it would be published before the end of the calendar year. I returned to Fort Bragg with the draft regulation and a commitment from them for $250,000.00 for the remainder of the year which I could start spending immediately. Probably the most important thing I got from them was that Special Forces Command would be treated equally with conventional Division Commands when it came to disbursing REDTRAIN funds.

Using the Department of the Army draft regulation as a guide, I wrote the 5th Special Forces Group REDTRAIN regulation which became the guideline for all Special Forces Group REDTRAIN regulations. I set up a REDTRAIN account with the 5th Special Forces Group comptroller, a Government Service (GS) civilian, and she assigned the accounting codes for disbursement. The training was valuable, and if I let the money be eaten by travel and lodging expenses, it wouldn't go very far and my soldiers would lose out on this very valuable training. So I started networking. I spent many hours on the phone, both day and night due to different time zones, coordinating modes of travel and lodging for my soldiers. Whenever possible, I would piggy-back a group of my people on Military transportation being used by other units who were going in our direction. I controlled the money to the penny. My reputation became such that I could walk into the comptroller's office and money would be allocated for whatever I wanted.

Things didn't always work out perfectly, though. There were two occasions when the Fort Bragg Finance and Accounting Office mucked things up regarding overseas trips. The first was a trip to Syria by one of my unit's teams and the other was a trip to Germany by my whole unit. The team ate the local food and was billeted in tents in the desert. The bean counters at the Finance and Accounting Office looked at this as being provided government rations and quarters. The married soldiers were notified that their rations and quarters allowance would be taken away for the period they were gone. This single act by the government was about to create an unfair and unnecessary hardship on the soldiers and their families. I went to Finance and initially ran into a brick wall. I ran into the "policy" dodge that whenever government rations and quarters are provided, regardless of what government, then a soldier's rations and quarters will be recovered by the U.S. government. When I showed the Finance Officer photos of the Syrian food and the living conditions of my soldiers, the order was rescinded and my soldiers' income wasn't affected. The second occasion was in early 1980 and involved a trip to Germany. This time the Fort Bragg Finance and Accounting Office froze future use of funds until receipts for lodging were produced. I went straight to the Finance Officer and showed him photos of our living conditions. Everyone, including the Unit Commander, lived in an attic that we had cleaned out when we arrived in Germany. We literally displaced the pigeons and turned the attic into a barracks with cots aligned in two rows. Funds were immediately released back to the 5th Special Forces Group comptroller.

THE DC MOTORCYCLE COP

Circa Early 1980. A new Commander came on board at the 400th Special Operations Detachment. Besides being Special Forces qualified, Captain C.J. McKee was also an Aviator. He preferred fixed-wing aircraft, but could also fly helicopters. We had a kinship of sorts because I wore an Aircraft Crewmember Badge on my uniform. I flew on one of his favorite aircraft, the RU21D which was a fixed-wing turbo-prop plane that cruised at 300 miles per hour (I could never get the hang of knots).

Captain McKee wanted to take the 400th SOD to Germany for Live Environment Training (LET) so the unit as a whole could participate in a real-world intelligence collection mission instead of each of the three assigned teams being fragmented toward different areas of operation. Since I was the 400th SOD Operations NCO, REDTRAIN NCO, and 5th Special Forces Group REDTRAIN Officer, he took me with him to the Pentagon. Captain McKee was going to meet with Major General Paul Menoher, the Deputy Chief of Staff for Intelligence, United States Army; and I was meeting with the U.S. Army REDTRAIN Officer. All the wheels were set in motion and the 400th Special Operations Detachment would be deployed to Augsburg, Germany.

We had a several hours left before our return flight to Fort Bragg, North Carolina. Captain McKee wanted to see the Lincoln Memorial, so we were off on a tour of Washington town. I was driving our rental car. We could see the Lincoln Memorial but couldn't get close because all we were doing was driving around in circles and I couldn't find a side street to get to it. I was finally within a block of the Memorial, still driving in circles, but couldn't find an entrance.

I was driving parallel to a row of ten-foot-high hedges when there was an entrance. Just a slight problem...there were two huge DO NOT ENTER signs on each side of the entrance. Nothing ventured, nothing gained. Go for it! I pulled in, took an immediate right turn, and came up behind a row of cars that were pulled over next to the hedge. Walking along the row from car to car were four DC Motorcycle Cops handing out traffic citations.

One of the DC Motorcycle Cops, about the size of a house, was walking toward our car. I was looking at Captain McKee and he was looking at me, and we were both thinking, "We're in deep kimchi!"

When the DC Motorcycle Cop arrived at my door, I said, "Excuse me, sir. We're on temporary duty from Fort Bragg and we need assistance."

His demeanor changed from law enforcer to helper of the lost. He asked, "Where are you trying to get to?"

I looked him square in the eye, pointed at the Lincoln Memorial just a quarter of a block away and said, "There."

The DC Motorcycle Cop looked at me and said, "Well then. I suggest you turn your car around, drive down to the river, park there, and walk back up here."

I thanked him for his assistance; we quickly exited, parked at the river and walked back to the Lincoln Memorial.

THE MARINE

This is the story of a United States Marine. He was a Gunnery Sergeant. I did not know him, but it was my honor to know his men. The place: Islamabad. The time: Perilous. Under today's Rules of Engagement, the Marine's actions would have earned him the Distinguished Service Cross; possibly the Medal of Honor. He was posthumously awarded the Legion of Merit for Valor. The Marine saved the lives of every American citizen and local national employee on the U.S. Embassy grounds.

When I arrived in Islamabad, the U.S. Embassy was being rebuilt and Embassy personnel were working out of the United Nations building. I had met the head of the UN delegation and his wife when I was in London, so it was easy for me to blend in. Additionally, one of my residences was next door to their house and my other residence was at the Holiday Inn.

I said before the time was perilous. There had been the Iran debacle and the slightest perceived infraction against the Muslim world could be disastrous. It happened. The Embassy was surrounded by 20,000 irate Muslims. The Embassy was burning.

The premier assignment for a U.S. Marine is Embassy duty. The best of the elite. Marine Guards represent the best qualities of an American citizen all over the world.

The Marine positioned his men in strategic defensive positions and he placed two men on the roof. He directed every living person to the "safe room" beneath the Embassy. Once they were secured, he had his men on the ground withdraw from their positions.

The Marine went onto the roof. As he arrived, one of his men was wounded by sniper fire. He told his other man to drop down to the floor below and he assisted the wounded man through the portal and lowered him to the waiting man. The Marine was instantly killed by sniper fire.

WHY I WAS IN PAKISTAN

Circa early August 1980 to early March 1981. I really don't know why I was selected to work with the Central Intelligence Agency. Maybe it was because I was in Iran, or because of something I had discovered about the Soviets and Cuba, or a couple of projects I worked on for the Defense Intelligence Agency, or projects with the National Security Agency, or maybe there was no one in particular in mind and my name was spit out of a computer. Regardless of the reason, a message came to Fort Bragg for me to report to the National Security Agency. I was then instructed to report to an office at the State Department. I complied with the instructions and was informed that any correspondence to me or about me would be directed to that office. I was then taken to the Central Intelligence Agency at Langley. There I met the Chief of the Division that would be controlling me. After in processing, anything associating me with the Military was secured in a safety deposit box, to include my ID card. I was issued a State Department ID.

My assignment was Islamabad, Pakistan. Politics at the national level wasn't my game. I knew politicians, only from briefings and social events. I was an Arabic speaking Special Operations Soldier with ties to Government Intelligence Agencies using a State Department billet who would be going to a U.S. Embassy in a foreign land. Sort of. The Embassy had been burned by 20,000 irate Muslims. Embassy personnel worked out of the UN building while a new Embassy was being built. I worked for the CIA Site Chief and we had an office in the secure part of the building. Only the Site Chief and Ambassador knew I was Military. And only the Site Chief knew I was Special Forces. If the Ambassador had known, I would have been persona-non-gratis.

It could be the reason I was selected for this job was that I grew up in Nebraska and the assumption was that I could ride a horse. When not within the border of Pakistan, riding a 12th century horse and looking up in the sky at a 20th century Hind is indescribable. Definitely an adrenaline rush. Especially when you know that the only thing between you and the devastating destruction that machine can produce is horse meat.

Mostly it was a day job and not many over nights. I had two residences. One was a house shared by Americans and the other was at the Islamabad Holiday Inn. I preferred the house because there was a live-in cook and he could make leather taste like filet mignon. He could have easily been a world-class chef. My favorite dish he prepared was the lasagna.

The Christmas holidays brought on many foreign embassy parties. I attended a few hosted by Americans, Europeans and Africans. The New Year rolled around and it was 1981. I was preparing to return to Washington when an incident happened. Since I was still on the clock, the mission was mine. There was a plane hijacking at Rawalpindi, the international airport outside Islamabad. So I spent the day at Rawalpindi. Before my arrival, the hijackers murdered a passenger. I don't know if they knew it or not, but he was a ranking Pakistani government official. The Pakistanis complied with the hijackers' demands. Then the plane just sat on the runway. All the while, I was doing my job. Then the plane took off. Time to wrap up. I sent a message to Washington and said the plane would land in Tehran in two hours. The plane landed in Tehran two hours later. Outside the hijackers, I was the only person on the planet who knew where the plane was headed. PK147 made international news.

The following day, I had a visitor from Washington. He had my hard copy Military personnel file with him. It was a known fact that hard copies of personnel files never left the Hoffman Building at Department of the Army. I had never seen my hard copy and here it was in front of me. I was impressed; not with my file, but that this guy had it. I was also offered a job. Starting salary $55,000.00 a year; ten year retirement program, the only stipulation was the first five years had to be overseas and I could choose the assignment. Bangkok was looking pretty good to me. This offer was overwhelming and I said I would provide an answer the following day. The answer was no. I'm a Soldier.

Every few years after that meeting, no matter where I was, someone would stop by my office and ask if I were interested in a new career. My final visit was in Panama.

It was time to go back to the States and back to the Army. When I returned to Langley and got the real me back, there was one more thing to do. I was going to be introduced to President Reagan. That was ten or fifteen seconds that lasted me a lifetime.

I returned to Fort Bragg, North Carolina. A couple things happened while I was gone. My staff position that had been temporarily filled was permanently filled. And, Department of the Army, in its infinite wisdom, had decided to select me for promotion. I returned to new assignment orders for Germany and I was a First Sergeant. I didn't even know what a First Sergeant was, but I was one.

A final note. While I was relaxing at home, there was something on the news that caught my attention. A plane hijacking in Bangkok. I watched the news footage with interest because I knew what was going on and there might be someone there who would get an opportunity to meet the President.

Except for cross-border forays, occasional late night into early morning jaunts, and the plane hijacking, I had what was for the most part a day job. Partly for relaxation, and mostly to stay in shape, I would run five to six miles at daybreak along the edge of the city. Sometimes I would run with the Marines. I think they were surprised that on old man in his early thirties could keep up with them. Especially a diplomat.

On one particular morning, I had crossed a small bridge, when I heard growling behind me. At the end of the bridge, was a pack of five or six hyenas that had come up the bank from a dry creek bed. Hyenas would come down out of the mountains to forage for food. Alone, they are timid, but in a pack, they're vicious. And they were interested in me.

On my left was an eight-foot high stone wall with broken glass on top and a little further forward was a double-wide iron gate. I beat feet for the gate with the hyenas in pursuit. When I reached the gate, I jumped up, grabbed the top, and pulled myself over. When I dropped to the ground, there was a group of women outside cooking near the corner of their house. They beckoned me over and took me inside their home. I was introduced to the men of the family and invited to stay for their version of coffee.

I was invited to come back later in the day for a family gathering, which I attended. The head of the household was a professor at the university and we became good friends while I was in Islamabad. We had many discussions about life in general and the applications of Islamic law.

One such discussion involved how thieves are punished and I explained to him that Westerners are bewildered that such harsh punishment is imposed. He explained that with the Muslim people, t he left hand touches food and is used primarily for eating. The right hand is used primarily for personal hygiene. Severing the right hand of a thief is the ultimate insult because he must then use his left hand for eating and taking care of personal hygiene. In addition, a thief will never steal with that hand again.

September 1981 through April 1983. My first assignment as a First Sergeant. I reported to the Headquarters, 302ⁿᵈ Military Intelligence Battalion, V Corps, United States Army Europe (USAREUR) at Frankfurt, Germany. After waiting all morning to meet the Battalion Sergeant Major, he did a quick meet and greet and told me the Battalion Commander wanted to meet me. So, I was introduced and the Sergeant Major departed. The Battalion Commander glanced at my assignment orders and told me my name looked familiar. Then he said, "Oh, I remember now. I sat on your promotion board, so I guess I deserve to get you." Honestly, I wasn't getting a real warm and fuzzy about this place.

The Battalion Commander told me that he didn't need a First Sergeant. However, a position just opened 100 miles away at Karlsruhe, Germany. The First Sergeant had been relieved of duty and he didn't think the Headquarters Company First Sergeant could handle the job in a line company. And then I walked through the door. So, if I was up to the challenge, the job was mine. I accepted. Then, he told me about the poor quality of Noncommissioned Officer leadership in the unit. And there was a coups-de-gras. The company barracks was on restriction because there had been a recent late-night disturbance and the installation staff duty officer had been thrown through a second story window. This was a lot of information to digest on a Friday morning. So, that afternoon I rented a car and drove the 100 miles to Gerszewski Barracks at Karlsruhe, Germany arriving after duty hours. I parked in front of the unit. It was time to meet my demons.

Wearing civilian clothes and my new gray London Fog topcoat I had purchased in London after I left Pakistan, I entered the building. In front of me, to my left, was the CQ (Charge-of-Quarters) sitting at a small desk watching television. I walked past him unchallenged and went up the stairwell toward the billeting area. When I reached the second floor, I opened the double doors at the billeting entrance and glanced inside. There was an NCO standing at one end of the hallway and another NCO at the other end. Again, I wasn't challenged. So, I went to the third floor. As I opened the double doors, a beer bottle went flying past and bounced along the floor in the hallway. Two

NCOs were standing together talking and one of them said, "Who the hell threw that?" Once again, I wasn't challenged. So, I went down stairs, exited the building, got into my rental car, and drove back to Frankfurt. Discipline sucked and there was a lot of work to do.

Monday morning. I was ready to go to work. I wore my BDUs (Battle Dress Uniform) with bloused, spit-shined Corcoran boots; subdued V Corps unit insignia and Special Forces combat insignia; and subdued pin-on metal CIB (Combat Infantryman Badge), Aircraft Crewmember Badge and Master Parachutist Badge. I had borrowed a jeep from the Battalion Headquarters Company First Sergeant at Frankfurt and drove to Karlsruhe. I met the new Company Commander outside the building. He had recently come on board and we entered together. The Commander was not acknowledged when he entered the building. Military courtesy sucked, too. We went to the Commander's office for a few minutes and then he introduced me to the Admin NCO. I signed a few documents and now belonged to a new Army home. Time to clean house.

The Admin NCO escorted me around the company area and introduced me to the Supply Sergeant and the Motor Sergeant. Then, I was shown my office which was across the hall from the Orderly Room. Just inside my office on the right, was a desk with a Senior NCO sitting at it. I asked her what her job was and she told me that she was the field first. Then I asked her what her job was before and she told me that she had been the Platoon Sergeant at the company remote site. I asked her about the current remote site Platoon Sergeant and she told me there wasn't one. I told her that yes there was and she was it. I didn't need a field first.

First order of business: Platoon Sergeant and Staff NCO meeting. Introductions, expectations and discipline. Everybody starts off with a clean slate. They as Senior Leaders have my backing and I expect them to back up their Junior NCOs. Be firm and fair, and treat people with respect and dignity. And I absolutely will not tolerate insubordination. Period. Next, I met with Squad Leaders and then, the junior enlisted soldiers assigned to the company. Key words were expectations and discipline, firm and fair, and respect and dignity. Once I got the matter of the barracks incident resolved, there would be a clean slate across the board. Open door policy and communication up and down the chain would be the key to success. The final order of business for Day One was a request for the three assigned lieutenants to meet me, at their leisure, in my office at 1700 (5:00 pm). The meeting was successful.

My company daily routine: Physical fitness training beginning at 0600; company formation at 0900; and normal duty hours until 1700. I didn't believe in GI parties. I set a basic attainable standard and expected the standard to be met. This applied all the time; even when we were being inspected by higher headquarters or during an IG (Inspector General) inspection. During my five and a half years as a First Sergeant and nearly ten years as a Sergeant Major, never was just only the minimum standard attained. Soldiers took pride in their work and living areas, in their unit, and most importantly, in themselves.

During the course of the next twelve months, much was attained. Morale was vastly improved, I had the best training program in the battalion, and I demanded and received the allocations to promote deserving Privates First Class to Specialist Fourth Class. Their drive, determination and desire would propel them to attain the rank of Sergeant. Nearly all of the Battalion Soldiers of the Month were my soldiers and every soldier I sent before a Battalion Promotion Board received a strong recommendation for promotion. All of my Junior NCOs attended the NCO Academy and I was able to get my Senior NCOs into the First Sergeant Course at Vilseck, Germany. I turned lemons into lemonade.

Late April 1983. I received a phone call from Major C.J. McKee, my commander a couple years earlier at Fort Bragg, North Carolina. He was taking command of an aviation company and wanted me as his First Sergeant. I told him I would be honored to take the job. So, my work was done at Karlsruhe and I was on my way to Kaiserslautern, Germany to attain bigger and better things and to make a new mark on history.

THE BULLY

Circa Late Fall 1981. My family was introduced to German "stairwell living." Our living quarters were located on the first floor of a three-story building that housed six families. The Military housing community we lived in was designated for Senior NCOs and their families. By 1981, Gracemary and I had four children. I was fortunate enough to be in the delivery room for each of my children. Matthew was now nine years old, Steven was seven, Dominic was five and Catherine was six months old. The American school for the boys was only a couple of blocks from our home and they walked to school together. They also easily made friends.

Matthew had a friend a year older and a little bigger. I'll call Matthew's friend Johnny. Little Johnny liked to use Matthew as a punching bag. Nothing serious; Matthew occasionally got in a few good licks himself. Johnny used to come over to our house to play all the time. The boys were really best friends. Whenever the boys were together, Gracemary kept an eye on them. Then one day, Gracemary was washing dishes at the kitchen sink and Matthew and Johnny were playing in the back yard. Gracemary was watching them through the kitchen window. Matthew and Johnny were talking, and Johnny said: "Matthew, I can't beat you up any more because your Dad is my Dad's First Sergeant." Matthew must have been ecstatic. Gracemary overheard this exchange between the boys. She said, "Johnny, that's ridiculous! You can beat up Matthew any time you want."

Special Forces soldiers are a unique breed. We would take care of our own. Rarely, if there were ever some type of disciplinary problem, would there be a reason for the chain-of-command to get involved. Other than the Law of Land Warfare, I knew nothing about Military Law or the Uniform Code of Military Justice (UCMJ) during my first sixteen years of Military service.

Then, the Army in its infinite wisdom decided to promote me to First Sergeant and send me to Germany. I was the Senior Enlisted Soldier of a 220-man ground tactical company and supposed to be the resident expert regarding discipline and the UCMJ. I didn't like what I saw. Looking around, it seemed that in conventional units, it was a badge of honor to convene courts-martial and administer nonjudicial punishment.

What I implemented was giving Noncommissioned Officers empowerment. They had the authority and I backed them up. It was a new experience for them. Initially, I bumped heads with a couple of lieutenants, but that issue was resolved very quickly. There was a new sheriff in town.

After dispensing with the disciplinary problems I inherited from the previous regime, the next 18 months as First Sergeant of a ground tactical company didn't require initiation of any legal action against a single soldier in my unit. Noncommissioned Officer leadership was the key. Lead by example. If one of my NCOs had a problem with a soldier committing a minor infraction, I encouraged their handling of the situation through corrective training. Situations dealt with included failure-to-repair (tardiness), personal appearance and uniform infractions, training issues, Military courtesy, and compliance with regulations and orders.

One example involved my own mail clerk who worked directly for me. I received a phone call from the manager of the local shoppette and she explained to me that she had asked him to remove his headgear inside the building. His response was that she was a civilian and he didn't have to listen to her. I explained to my mail clerk the error of his ways, and besides an apology, he would post himself at the entrance to the shoppette for two hours a night for the next five nights to remind people to remove their headgear when entering the building. After the initial ribbing by his friends the first two nights, he did an excellent job enforcing that portion of the Army uniform regulation.

When his corrective training was finished, I asked him what he had learned from the experience. His response was: "Well, First Sergeant, I learned that officers can be real asses!"

May 1983 through July 1984. My second assignment as a First Sergeant.

"First Sergeant for the 330ᵗʰ Electronic Warfare Aviation Company (Forward), 2ⁿᵈ Military Intelligence Battalion (Aerial Exploitation), 207ᵗʰ Military Intelligence Group (Combat Electronic Warfare Intelligence), VII Corps, United States Army Europe (USAREUR) responsible for the execution of the Joint Chiefs of Staff (JCS) directed Peacetime Airborne Reconnaissance Program (PARPRO) mission flown in direct support of VII Corps, USAREUR and United States Air Forces Europe (USAFE) tactical commanders."

The preceding was the first half of the introduction to the description of duties on my annual evaluation report. The second half of the introduction was: "Responsible for the career development, counseling and well-being of eighty-six Senior NCOs and seventy-nine enlisted soldiers. Provides command support through a key NCO support chain; insuring soldier development, quality of life and execution of the unit's mission. The Senior NCO of a 189 soldier company spread over 70 kilometers, operating from three locations."

What wasn't mentioned in the introduction was that my aviation company also had 24 pilots assigned, both officer and warrant officer. A little over a year earlier, the newly designated Company Commander, Major C.J. McKee, asked me to be his First Sergeant and he wanted his pilots to be able to operate and survive under combat conditions both on the ground and in the air. That's where I came in. Combat experience both on the ground and in the air and tactical expertise.

When I arrived at the 330ᵗʰ EW Aviation Company, I already had over a year and a half First Sergeant experience and I knew the administrative things that needed to be done and I had points of contact at USAREUR and Department of the Army to circumvent red tape. One thing that I became quite adept at over the years was making the system work or circumventing it altogether. I immediately implemented the soldier and NCO programs that I had in place at my previous unit. Initially, taking care of soldiers was my primary concern. Those soldiers that specifically needed Military education and leadership training went to the top of the list and I got them into the programs they needed. Those Senior NCOs who strived to become First Sergeants were enrolled in the First Sergeant Course at Vilseck, Germany.

To get the ball rolling, I requested that each Platoon Sergeant provide me with the names of soldiers who were having payroll problems. I went to the Kaiserslautern Finance Office and sat down with the Noncommissioned Officer in Charge to resolve each problem for each soldier. Next, I wanted to know if there were any family issues that would affect duty performance. I didn't want a soldier scheduled for deployment if his wife would be going into labor in his absence or if there was an illness at home and nobody would be there to take care of a sick child or spouse. Family first.

There was a Senior NCO in my company that didn't have a job. He hadn't attended any of my meetings and he just seemed to hang around. I looked his name up on the unit roster and he was being carried as excess. I asked him to come to my office. He told me that he was an alcoholic. The previous regime had command-directed him to the Community Alcohol Abuse Prevention and Control Program and his primary duty responsibilities after that were ash and trash details. He had zero responsibility. Previously, he was the Platoon Sergeant at the company remote site and the straw that broke the camel's back with his drinking was that he was discovered passed out inside a dumpster. I asked him how he was doing in the program. He told me that he hadn't had a drink in four months. I told him that his ash and trash days were over and that he was now the Headquarters Platoon Sergeant. All the people that worked in Operations, the Orderly Room, the Supply Room, the Motor Pool and I belonged to him.

A strong Noncommissioned Officer Chain of Command is tantamount to the success of any Military organization. Officers provide guidance and NCOs get the job done. Coming up through the ranks in Special Forces, I saw how NCOs make things happen. The key is leadership, communication, and accountability. I set up the rating chain. All Platoon Sergeants were rated by me. Platoon Leaders were the senior raters and the Company Commander was the report reviewer. Neat and simple. As far as company staff, the Headquarters Platoon Sergeant rated Section Leaders, I was the senior rater and the

Company Commander was the report reviewer. Everything was in place. Leadership, communication and accountability.

Major McKee's dream for a tactical Field Training Exercise (FTX) was about to become a reality. It had taken a month to get requisitions approved for general purpose canvas tents from the 21st Support Command. Formal joint-service requisitions and back-channel Senior NCO coordination affected a rapid resolution for use of a designated area at Ramstein Air Force Base, Kaiserslautern, Germany. We had an airplane hanger, approved air corridors, and an open field to set up the tents. Major McKee wanted a pilot hot-bedding sleep area near the hanger and he also worked himself into the pilot mission rotations. I drove to the 2nd MI Battalion Headquarters at Pirmesans, Germany and hand-carried an immediate change to my weekly training schedule and handed it to the Sergeant Major. It was 6:00 pm on Friday, a light rain was starting, and I started my return trip from Pirmesans back to Kaiserslautern. I was sipping on a canned Coke and when I set it down on the console, it tipped over. I reached for the can and swerved slightly. The inside of my car was completely absorbed by blue light. I watched the MP approach my car in the rear view mirror. It probably didn't help matters when I told him that I spilled my drink. The field sobriety test was a breeze. I'm just glad I wasn't as uncoordinated as I usually am. And, this guy had absolutely no sense of humor. I offered him a can of Coke before leaving and he didn't appreciate the gesture. Once again I started my return trip. The upcoming exercise was totally controlled by NCOs.

At midnight, the Commander, Executive Officer, the Platoon Sergeants and I met at the Company Headquarters. We went over the sequence of events and at 0100 I told the Charge of Quarters to initiate Company Alert Procedures. At 0200 the 330th Electronic Warfare Aviation Company (Forward) had 100% accountability.

At 0400 United States Army Europe (USAREUR) initiated a Command Alert. Immediately, I responded with 100% accountability. USAREUR asked for clarification and again I responded with 100% accountability. No unit in the history of USAREUR had ever immediately responded to a USAREUR Alert with 100% accountability. We had bragging rights.

This story started with the description of duties on my annual evaluation report. I'm going to end it with the comments written by the Rater, Major Claude J. McKee, Company Commander; and Indorser, Lieutenant Colonel Dempsey L. Malaney, Battalion Commander. Occasionally, there was duplication of thought, so I combined their comments in those areas to maintain an even flow.

"First Sergeant Carden is the most outstanding Senior NCO ever assigned as First Sergeant. He is an outstanding Noncommissioned Officer who performs all duties in a very competent and professional manner. Upon assuming the First Sergeant position, he immediately made his mark as a firm, competent leader and infused his driving enthusiasm and discerning judgment into the Noncommissioned Officer Chain to breathe new vitality into the company's mission accomplishments and Noncommissioned Officer Development programs. First Sergeant Carden has made key improvements in this unit's overall performance as recognized by Battalion, Group and Corps Sergeant Majors. He has provided powerful dedication and evoked spontaneous esprit de corps. First Sergeant Carden was responsible for a soldier within this command winning battalion, 21st Support Command and USAREUR Soldier of the Year. Soldier appearance, military bearing and common skills proficiency have markedly improved under his leadership. He has expended no less than 100% effort to improve the soldiers' quality of life to include appearance of work areas, barracks living conditions and off duty recreational programs. He has developed an environment in which NCOs strive to excel. The leadership provided by First Sergeant Carden resulted in an unprecedented number of soldiers attending the Primary Leadership Development Course and the First Sergeant Course. First Sergeant Carden did a superb job in planning and deploying his company on a tactical field training exercise, a task that has not been achieved for three years. His loyalty and dedication are unsurpassed. First Sergeant Carden exemplifies the title "First Sergeant" and has been a very positive example to be emulated by all soldiers."

The preceding paragraph was the combined evaluation from a yellowed 25-year-old official document. Recommendations regarding potential and future assignments included promotion to Sergeant Major, selection for the Sergeants Major Academy, appointment as a Command Sergeant Major, and assignments at Battalion and Brigade level. All of those things happened within six years. Plus, my final Military assignment was at a Major Army Command (MACOM).

My one year assignment at the 330th EW Aviation Company resulted in the award of a Meritorious Service Medal. Unprecedented for a one year assignment. Next on the agenda, the 10th Special Forces Group (Airborne), Fort Devens, Massachusetts.

GUARDRAIL WINE

The 330th Electronic Warfare Aviation Company conducted daily operations from three locations spread out over a 70 kilometer area. We were responsible for collecting real-time/real-world Signals Intelligence (SIGINT) in Europe during the Cold War. Our marching orders came directly from the Joint Chiefs of Staff (JCS) to fulfill requirements of the Peacetime Airborne Reconnaissance Program (PARPRO).

My Company Headquarters was located at Kaiserslautern, Germany; aircraft were located at Ramstein Air Force Base; and I had a remote intelligence collection site located in the middle of a wine vineyard in the picturesque German countryside.

Our unit designation was GUARDRAIL. Since we conducted our actual war time mission every day, there were a lot of eyes on us. Political eyes. At least once a quarter, especially around holidays, we would have distinguished visitors who were either Senators or Congressmen or Congresswomen.

It seemed there was always a general officer or a politician that wanted to visit the remote site. The Platoon Sergeant was in charge and remote site duty for my soldiers was a plush assignment. Living conditions weren't quite to Military standard. A German four-poster was cheap money and some soldiers preferred to sleep in the comfort of a two-foot thick mattress instead of a Military bed. As long as soldiers maintained their Military clothing and equipment, I wasn't concerned with how they counted sheep at night. There was a brigadier or major general that visited once and when he saw the living conditions, he went ballistic. He said that soldiers in his command would only sleep on government issued bedding. I cleaned his comments up quite a bit. They were actually in reference to a certain type of French house. He instructed one of his aides to take notes and submit requisitions. I talked to the Corps Sergeant Major about keeping generals away from my remote site. Besides, the politicians loved it.

I mentioned earlier that the remote site was located in a wine vineyard. We had our own label. It was White Zinfandel. The label was "GUARDRAIL" with a circular picture of our aircraft on it. I am not a drinker. But I would occasionally sip our wine. It was delicious, if that's how you can describe a wine. I also mentioned holidays. It seems we had a lot of visitors who seemed to deplete our wine stock around Christmas time.

The Services have programs to recognize service members who take that extra step to excel. The Army has Soldier of the Month at company and battalion levels, Soldier of the Quarter and Year at battalion and brigade level, and Soldier of the Year at corps and major command level. In some overseas commands, soldiers are recognized for excellence at the community level. The programs are competitive and stress the soldiers' knowledge in the Military sciences and current events.

My Electronic Warfare (EW) Aviation Company Headquarters was located at Kaiserslautern, Germany. I received a phone call from the installation Sergeant Major asking if I would sit on a Community Soldier of the Quarter Board. I said sure, he gave me my subjects for questions, and told me the board would convene in an hour.

I had recently accepted this First Sergeant position, my new unit had never previously participated in community events, and this was what I thought would be a chance to get involved. After the final soldier appeared, I said that I didn't know about anyone else, but I felt this had been a waste of my time and the other members of the board. The soldiers appearing were ill-prepared and if we selected one of them to represent our community at USAREUR (United States Army Europe), it would be an embarrassment to the community. I asked the Sergeant Major if I could have my new Soldier of the Month, a wheeled vehicle mechanic, appear before the board. He said that he agreed with my conclusion and that he had no problem with my soldier appearing. Then the other First Sergeants asked if they could also have their soldiers appear. So, phone calls were made and the board adjourned and reconvened two hours later.

I don't know how the original soldiers were selected to appear before the board, but four First Sergeants of tenant units brought in their best soldiers. All the soldiers did well and represented their units well. My soldier outshined everyone and was selected as the Kaiserslautern Community Soldier of the Quarter.

Specialist Fourth Class Carl Laksmannen was probably one of the best young soldiers I have ever met. He was a wheeled vehicle mechanic (Jeeps and trucks), he had a thirst for knowledge, intense focus, and he had excellent Military bearing. I think what impressed me most about him was that he showed respect to every person he met. He religiously wrote letters home to his family and I believe he also provided financial assistance to his parents. Carl Laksmannen was the perfect son.

Specialist Laksmannen performed his assigned Military duties during duty hours. During non-duty hours, he studied Military regulations and current events. I set up mock boards consisting of my Platoon Sergeants and myself for him to appear before. The center seat at the table was left empty and I placed an 8x10 Chain-of-Command photo of the Battalion Sergeant Major in front of the empty seat so he would be comfortable answering questions and talking to that face. Since he was my Soldier of the Month, he qualified for appearance at the Battalion Soldier of the Month competition at Pirmasens.

The Battalion Soldier of the Month and Quarter boards were won by Specialist Laksmannen. His packet was submitted for the USAREUR competition. Somewhere in the mix, Specialist Laksmannen also appeared before the 21st Support Command Soldier of the Year competition because he was the Kaiserslautern Soldier of the Quarter. He was selected as the 21st Support Command Soldier of the Year. I was approached by a Sergeant Major from VII Corps who presented me with a proposition. I told him that I would discuss it with Specialist Laksmannen and get back to him. After consultation with my Sergeant Major, I approached Specialist Laksmannen with the proposition. There was a once in a lifetime opportunity for Specialist Laksmannen if he should decide to accept. I explained to him what I thought would be the pros and cons. He decided to go for it. So, Specialist Laksmannen was on the road to competing in two concurrent Soldier of the Year competitions. The first competition was for the United States Army Europe and the second was for the Association of the United States Army (AUSA) USAEUR. So Specialist Laksmannen would be competing against what was considered the best soldiers in the United States Army assigned to the European Theater which included Europe, North Africa and the Middle East. This was a heavy burden for a 20-year-old Army wheeled-vehicle mechanic.

When it was all over, Specialist Laksmannen was selected as both the United States Army Europe Soldier of the Year and the Association of the United States Army USAREUR Soldier of the Year. These events happened in 1983-1984 and Specialist Laksmannen's achievements have never been duplicated.

Specialist Carl Laksmannen is the reason I became deeply involved in soldier programs. I wrote and continuously updated two study guides that helped young soldiers and noncommissioned officers prepare for competitive boards and promotion boards. When I opened the United States Army Military Intelligence School Noncommissioned Officer Academy at Fort Devens, Massachusetts about five years later, I provided copies of my study guides to those NCOs who wanted to take them back to their units. Eventually, there were copies distributed world-wide.

August 1984 to July 1985. After a highly successful European tour of duty with two consecutive First Sergeant positions, I was reassigned to the 10th Special Forces Group at Fort Devens, Massachusetts. Technically, I was coming home. Gracemary could see her parents and my children would be near their grandparents. And I could return to the 402nd Special Operations Detachment. It was a win-win situation all around. Things don't always turn out the way we want. The 10th Group Command Sergeant Major had other plans for me. The Special Forces Groups were scheduled by Department of the Army to undergo reorganization and the support units would be aligned under their own battalion. The new battalion needed a Sergeant Major and I was it. As with many positions in the Army, this was a case of having a position and authority, but not actually having the rank. I was designated the Battalion Sergeant Major.

Support Battalion (Airborne) (Provisional), 10th Special Forces Group (Airborne), 1st Special Forces became a reality. On paper anyway. On day one, two people were assigned to the battalion. The Commander, Lieutenant Colonel Vernon Leyde and the Command Sergeant Major, Master Sergeant David C. Carden. We had carte blanche to staff our Battalion Headquarters and we were to be completely operational in 30 days. The new battalion consisted of Headquarters and Headquarters Company, Service Company, Signal Company, and the Military Intelligence Company. We accomplished our mission in record time and Department of the Army approved our existence.

Lieutenant Colonel Leyde and I were sent to Fort Bragg, North Carolina to assist with organizing the Support Battalion, 5th Special Forces Group. We spent about two weeks at Fort Bragg and then returned to Fort Devens. Special Forces now had another battalion modeled after ours and the rest of the Special Forces Groups would soon follow.

The Noncommissioned Officer Development Program (NCODP) that I developed was very thorough and comprehensive. The Soldier Programs that I created in Germany were put in place. I established an open communication channel with officers, NCOs and soldiers of the battalion. This created trust. There was no "we-they" or "us-them" mind set. Separate entities that each supported the 10th Special Forces Group were brought together under a single umbrella and we became a cohesive unit. I convened a Soldier of the Quarter Board and selected a radio teletype operator from Signal Company to represent the Battalion at the Group Soldier of the Quarter Board. I provided him training and assistance to prepare for his appearance before the Group Sergeant Major's board. He was selected as the Group Soldier of the Quarter. He then competed against the best from the United States Army Intelligence School, the Medical Command, the Engineer Command, and the Reserve Forces Command. My radio teletype operator who had never had any exposure like this in his life was selected as the Post Soldier of the Quarter and went on to become the 1984 Fort Devens Soldier of the Year. I had the ability to recognize a spark and turn it into a burning inferno. Helping soldiers succeed continued into 1985. Sergeant Major Lee Fondas arrived from Germany and Department of the Army reassigned me to the United States Army Intelligence School, Fort Devens. I was about to embark on a whole new journey. Creating young soldiers.

Circa August 1985 to December 1986. I dusted off my First Sergeant stripes and pinned them back on. By the time I finished this assignment, I served as a First Sergeant for five and one half years. When I met the Battalion Commander and Sergeant Major, they welcomed me on board. This encounter was a 180 degree turn-around from my first assignment as a First Sergeant. The company I was getting had a few problems. There wasn't currently a Commander and a new one would be on board in about a week. And by the way, the First Sergeant had just been relieved. This situation was eerily similar to my first assignment as a First Sergeant. Oh well, time to go to work.

Now I was the First Sergeant of 200 trainees and I was responsible for their billeting, training, health and welfare. I met my cadre and told them that I would like to make a few alterations to the building to help us run a more efficient company. I showed them my plan that I had drawn up and everyone was on board. The first thing I did was to have the office, supply and administrative areas shifted from a secluded end of the ground floor to the center of the building near the front and rear doors that were opposite each other. Anyone entering the building would have immediate access to the command element. The offices that were vacated each had a private bathroom with shower. I turned them into one and two soldier billeting areas. They would be a prize for those trainees who exceeded standards.

I walked into a competitive environment. The First Sergeants in the other three companies vied for bragging rights as the monthly Battalion Honor Company. They were all spit and polish and their Drill Sergeants were tough task masters. The leader of the pack was A Company. As you entered the building, the first thing you saw was a trophy case with a bunch of Honor Company trophies. I don't think my new company had a trophy case, let alone any trophies. Yep, it was spit and polish. People were walking around with pads on their boots so as not to scratch or mar the floors. I was almost afraid to walk on their shiny floors. But what the heck. I did anyway.

My new unit was B Company, 1st Battalion, 2nd School Brigade, United States Army Intelligence School Devens, Fort Devens, Massachusetts. I had a Charge of Quarters (CQ) desk positioned at the center of the hallway with access to the front and rear entrances. This desk was manned 24 hours a day. People were greeted when they entered the building and when officers who outranked the Commander and Sergeants Major entered, the whole building knew because their presence was announced. The Commander's office and mine were next to each other and each office was accessed from the hallway. The Commander and I also had a door connecting our offices that I had installed. My first order of business was to sit down with the Commander, Captain Anthony G. Kaliher. He turned out to be one of the finest young officers with whom I had ever served. Captain Kaliher had been in the battalion for a short while. But during that time, he had been receiving razzing from the other commanders about the Honor Company thing. I told him not to worry about it.

My Drill Sergeants were all Staff Sergeants; two male and two female. My Supply Sergeant was also a Staff Sergeant and my Orderly Room was run by a Sergeant who had two clerks working for him. What I ascertained from that first meeting was that my cadre wanted support and guidance. They knew how to train and lead, they just wanted someone to back them up. They could count on me. Now, what did I want? I wanted soldiers to be treated with respect and dignity. All I required was that soldiers meet a basic standard when it came to personal appearance and personal living areas. I didn't believe in GI parties and we would never have one regardless of the circumstances. I set the standards and those soldiers who didn't meet them would receive corrective training. Those soldiers who exceeded the standards would be appropriately recognized and rewarded. Now, about that Honor Company thing....

My company won Battalion Honor Company that first month. Then it was neck and neck between the A Company First Sergeant and me the next seven months. His company won four times and my company won three more times. However, my soldiers were selected as the Battalion Soldier of the Month for eight consecutive months. My soldiers also won two Battalion Soldier of the Quarter boards for two consecutive quarters; and one soldier was selected as the Brigade Soldier of the Quarter. A trainee won the title over all the assigned soldiers in the School Brigade to include permanent party soldiers. It all ended for me at the eight month mark. The final week of March

1986, my trainees and Drill Sergeants were transferred to the other companies and on April Fools Day, I reopened as a Noncommissioned Officer Student Company.

The U.S. Army Training and Doctrine Command (TRADOC) wanted all Army schools for Noncommissioned Officers to be run the same as NCO Academies. So, that final week of March 1986, I travelled to the NCO Academies at Fort Dix, New Jersey and Fort Gordon, Georgia. I wanted to incorporate the best qualities of those two institutions into my NCO Academy. Administratively, my Standard Operating Procedures (SOP) and soldier programs would remain the same with a few minor adjustments. I had been using the same basic guidelines I had written when I took over my first company. Through the years, they had gotten better and now it was just a matter of adapting to a new environment. Time I spent with the Commandants was well served. Not only did I get some good ideas from them, but they also kept some of my ideas for themselves.

My new cadre were experienced instructors from the Intelligence School. They each volunteered to work for me. I suppose that I had gained a reputation as being a fair and professional Noncommissioned Officer. I gladly welcomed them on board. My company now had to be evaluated and accredited by TRADOC. Until B Company became accredited, we were a "provisional" NCO Academy. Let the festivities begin.

Until 1986, Noncommissioned Officer and Warrant Officer courses of instruction were considered "gentlemen's courses." The Noncommissioned Officer Education System (NCOES) was implemented. Incorporated into NCOES were NCO Academy standards. I was now First Sergeant of a Noncommissioned Officer Student Company consisting of over 300 soldiers undergoing Basic Noncommissioned Officer Course (BNCOC), Advanced Noncommissioned Officer Course (ANCOC) and Warrant Officer Certification Training (WOCT) in twenty career developing courses of instruction. My new students were wary. They were career Noncommissioned Officers who were being thrust into an NCO Academy environment. To make matters worse, their new First Sergeant, just a week before, was running what amounted to a Basic Training unit. The rumors were running rampant. Once they saw me at our first formation, some of them felt much better because they had worked for me before. They were the NCOs I counted on to make things run smoothly from within. I let everyone know they would be treated with the respect their rank deserved. The Senior NCOs would be billeted in the one and two person rooms and all other NCOs would be billeted in the four person rooms. I told them what I expected as far as adherence to standards and that my cadre and I looked forward to attending their graduations.

Mentoring was what I considered my most important job in this arena. I was in a position to develop future senior leaders in the United States Army. It was something I wasn't going to let go to waste. I did my best. One of my cadre and nine of my students were selected consecutively as the Battalion NCO of the Month. And one of my students was the Brigade NCO of the Quarter. TRADOC certified my company in nine months and B Company would officially become the U.S. Army Intelligence School Noncommissioned Officer Academy on February 1st, 1987. The Standard Operating Procedures that I wrote would be the bedrock of the Academy. My First Sergeant position would be upgraded to Commandant. A position held by a Sergeant Major. I was moving on to bigger and better things. The Department of the Army, once again in its infinite wisdom, had selected me to attend the U.S. Army Sergeant Major Academy, and by the way, I would also be promoted to Sergeant Major sometime in the near future.

The NCO Academy phase of my career was over. I shall end this with a quote from my Senior Rater, Lieutenant Colonel Thomas E. Hanlon, extracted from my efficiency report: "First Sergeant Carden epitomizes the leadership standards of a senior noncommissioned officer. He does lead by example and he does exceptionally well. I have indeed noted a quantum improvement in the climate of command since First Sergeant Carden's assumption of duty. The NCOs and the soldiers undergoing training have adopted pride, integrity, loyalty and exceptional military bearing as their standard. They accept nothing less and First Sergeant Carden is responsible for that attitude and motivation. First Sergeant Carden is a leader, teacher, mentor and First Sergeant in every sense. The transformation in NCO training from pure academics to a professionally demanding NCO development program has been dramatic, productive and outstanding. First Sergeant

Carden is responsible for that transformation. He instituted incentive programs that raised every measurable standard of soldierization – fitness, pride, appearance, bearing and a sense of purpose in being a confident noncommissioned officer. Always caring, understanding and available, he guided and assisted subordinates in time of need. Numerous student NCOs have communicated to me directly that their goal is to emulate the image of a professional NCO to the degree demonstrated by First Sergeant Carden. On several occasions, for weeks at a time, he fulfilled the role of Battalion and Brigade Command Sergeant Major. His performance was impeccable and demonstrative of an experienced Command Sergeant Major."

THE BUONO PLAN

The opportunity to mold young people into good soldiers is the dream job in the Army. It is fulfilling and provides lifelong memories. Although you don't play favorites, there is always one soldier you want to see succeed more than anything. For me, that soldier was Private Buono. He was a big teddy bear and from day one of training, Private Buono was entered into the Weight Control Program and a program to build upper body strength because he couldn't do a single pull-up or a proper push-up.

My Drill Sergeants, in my opinion, were the best Drill Sergeants assigned to the U.S. Army Intelligence School. Staff Sergeant Glenda Story was a Brigade NCO of the Quarter. Her husband, Sergeant First Class Reginald Story, received a Warrant Officer appointment and I was honored with rendering his first salute.

Private Buono was assigned to Drill Sergeant Story's platoon. She put together a plan to build Private Buono's upper body strength and added a little something extra. I was walking to my office when I heard a voice behind me. "One, First Sergeant! Two, First Sergeant! The counting continued. I stopped, turned around and walked down the hallway to Private Buono. I looked down at Private Buono, who was in the push-up position on the floor, and I asked, "Private Buono, what are you doing?" He responded with, "Push-ups, First Sergeant!" I told him to recover, he jumped to the position of attention, and I asked him why he was doing push-ups. His response was, "Drill Sergeant Story told me that every time I see the First Sergeant, I have to drop and do ten push-ups." "It's the Buono Plan, First Sergeant." My response was, "I see. Carry-on Private Buono." At which point, he dropped down and started doing push-ups again. I stopped him and told him to continue with what he was going to do before he saw me. Staff Sergeant Story and my other Drill Sergeants were observing this exchange and were quite pleased with the results.

Private Buono had initiative. He also took it upon himself to do push-ups for his instructors as well. At the beginning and end of each academic day, he did push-ups in the classroom.

For the next few months, I would periodically hear Private Buono's voice in the distance as he was counting-out push-ups. I couldn't see him because he was on the ground and I would shout out, "Recover, Private Buono." At which point, the counting would stop. When Private Buono graduated from his Advanced Individual Training, he was technically proficient, met weight standards and was physically fit.

THE ONE-HANDED SNOW SHOVEL

Although it was a treat to have young soldiers like Private Buono in my training company, there were periodically soldiers who presented a leadership challenge. One such soldier was a malingerer. He knew how to play the system and he was quite good at malingering. Sometimes he didn't have the best of judgment. He was infatuated with one of the female trainees and she wanted nothing to do with him. This young private was absent from an early evening work detail and he missed a follow-up roll call. After the detail was finished, with all the drama of a soap opera, the missing private came stumbling through the building entrance and collapsed on the floor. Medical personnel were summoned and it was determined he had hypothermia.

A few days before, there was a snow storm. The malingerer had laid down in a snow bank to freeze himself to death. The only problem was, it was about fifty degrees and the snow was melting. All he really did was get wet.

Because he missed the work detail, he was subject to nonjudicial punishment and part of that punishment would be working for me for a few days. I chalked the snow bank incident up to just being stupid. With all the snow that we had, there was snow to be shoveled. The malingerer knew what was coming. When I informed him he would be working for me, he looked me in the eye and said, "That's ok First Sergeant. I'll go to the dispensary and get a profile for my wrist. I won't be able to shovel snow." I told him to attend his daily training and to see me after duty hours.

I called the JAG (Judge Advocate General) who is the military equivalent of a lawyer. In my case, a prosecutor. I asked if I could legally make a soldier shovel snow with a dust pan. I needed an answer before close of business. A couple hours later, the JAG walked into my office and handed me a letter. It was an official legal ruling that moving snow with a dust pan wasn't cruel or unusual punishment and that said dust pan was determined to be "a one-handed snow shovel." I asked him if he was sure because he would likely be getting a phone call from the Inspector General. He told me I was on solid legal ground. I thanked him and waited for close of business.

The malingerer wasn't happy, but he did his one-handed snow

shoveling for two days. On the third day, I received a phone call from Major General Menoher, the Commander of the U.S. Army Intelligence School at Fort Huachuca, Arizona. He told me that he had a visit from his Inspector General about trainee abuse. It seems the IG on my end jumped the gun and didn't check all the facts before elevating a complaint to our higher headquarters. I apologized to General Menoher for his being bothered with such a trivial matter, but I had in my possession a legal ruling that a dust pan was a one-handed snow shovel. With the official business out of the way, he asked me how my family was doing and I asked him for an update on his family. We had known each other for many years. When I retired nine years later, I had asked Lieutenant General Paul Menoher, Deputy Chief of Staff for Intelligence, United States Army to be the presiding official at my official retirement ceremony at Fort Bragg, North Carolina.

The training day ended and all the trainees had eaten their dinner. The malingerer reported to my office with a smile on his face. It quickly disappeared when I handed him his one-handed snow shovel and told him to get to work.

My final official duty of the day was to make an entry into my planning calendar to visit the Inspector General the next morning.

THE COORS NORTHEASTERN

Circa Fall 1986. My thoughts for running an NCO Academy were quite basic. Treat people with respect and dignity; and lead by example stressing fitness, pride, appearance, bearing and a sense of purpose in being a confident Noncommissioned Officer.

The very first class for the Intelligence School NCO Academy was formed in the summer of 1986. Two of my students were on Army softball championship teams. A female Sergeant was an All Army Fast Pitch Softball pitcher and a male Staff Sergeant was an All Okinawa second baseman. I posted a sign-up sheet for the Fort Devens fast pitch and slow pitch softball tournaments. My teams were filled almost immediately and I officially entered both tournaments. I was the team manager for both teams and back-up pitcher for the slow pitch team. My pitching provided comic relief for my students. During a ten day period, we won both tournaments and were officially Post Champions.

The Post slow pitch softball championship was a stepping stone to another tournament. Fort Devens was sponsoring the Coors Northeastern Slow Pitch Softball Tournament and the Post Sergeant Major was making it happen. The tournament was a one day event and would take place the following Saturday morning beginning at 0900.

On the Military side, there was quite a turn-out of spectators. Soldiers and family members from all the units at Fort Devens were there to provide support. No matter what the outcome, it was looking to be a fun day. The other teams started showing up. I think there were ten other teams. The tournament would take place at the three ball fields near the Verbeck Gate on the Ayer side of Fort Devens.

My team was scheduled in the first round and we won by default. The team that we were supposed to play against was a no show. Already in first place! The real test came an hour later. I was our starting pitcher and the first batter came to the plate. My strategy was to not show the other team my best stuff until maybe the third inning. The batter connected with my first pitch on the sweet spot of his bat and slammed the ball straight back into my glove. The impact knocked me down and the ball rolled out of my glove down the back of the pitcher's mound. I rolled over once, grabbed the ball and from a sitting position threw the ball to first base for the first out. Although the ball landed in the palm of my hand, the force of the impact broke three bones in the back of my hand. My pitching career ended on that dirt mound.

We placed third in the tournament. Appearances are deceiving. Most of the players on the other teams were over weight, ran slow and appeared to be out of breath by the time they reached first base. But it didn't matter. All they knew how to do was to hit home runs; or as in my case, an occasional bone cruncher. Speaking of which, my hand was secured to an aluminum soup bowl for the next four weeks.

One final note: Although it was a Coors softball tournament, there weren't any alcoholic beverages on the playing fields.

Circa January 1987 to October 1991. The Provisional NCO Academy was the closest I ever got to running an NCO Academy. But the organization I formed was run by Sergeant Major James Kelly, a good friend of mine, and he ran the Academy the way I had envisioned. Things have a way of working out for the best.

The United States Army Intelligence School is the premier assignment in the United States Army. My whole career to this point was in the tactical arena or training soldiers. Now I was in an academic environment. However, my first assignment was not in one of the academic departments. I was selected as the Intelligence School Secretariat Sergeant Major. My primary responsibility was providing leadership to a 220-person directorate. Elements under my control were the Military Police (MP), personnel security and investigations, logistics, a complex parking and snow removal plan, coordinating with contractors, inventory and ADP systems.

I helped one of the MPs prepare for the company Soldier of the Month board. After the board and a little more help in preparation, the MP won the battalion board and went on to be selected as the Brigade Soldier of the Quarter. At the same time, I helped a Noncommissioned Officer to become the Brigade NCO of the Quarter. During the next quarter, I helped another soldier who went through the process and was also selected as the Brigade Soldier of the Quarter. One of my former female Drill Sergeants asked me if I would help her prepare for the Drill Sergeant of the Year competition. I told her that I would gladly help. Sergeant First Class Jackie Moate was selected as the School Brigade Drill Sergeant of the Year. In 1991, I was a member of the Department of the Army promotion board that selected her for promotion to Master Sergeant.

I was getting closer to the academic departments. There was a four month stint as the Sergeant Major for the Directorate of Training and Doctrine. Then things changed.

In July 1988, The Sergeant Major for the Deputy Assistant Commandant (DAC) retired. The DAC Sergeant Major was second in power after the Intelligence School Sergeant Major. The Deputy Assistant Commandant, who was also Deputy Commander, would make the selection for his Sergeant Major. There were five directorate Sergeants Major including me plus four other Sergeants Major in the Command; and I was the most junior Sergeant Major at the Intelligence School and at Fort Devens. Since I'm writing this story about a powerful position, then the assumption would be that I was selected for that position. The assumption is correct.

Nearly a year and a half at the Intelligence School and I still didn't have an academic department. But here I was, the Deputy Assistant Commandant Sergeant Major supervising the conduct of training of three 240-person academic departments and a 291-person training development directorate. I also coordinated with Army Major Commands (MACOM) for personnel requirements in support of systems development and testing. And I represented the Command in the absence of the Intelligence School Command Sergeant Major. My plate was full, but I could rarely be found in my office. I was in the classrooms. The 1,500 students being trained daily were the primary reason we were there and I continually evaluated the conduct of training.

One of my primary duties was to ensure that trainees were treated properly and that they received quality training. If students were struggling with the instruction, I made it clear that they would receive whatever additional training that was needed to meet the standards for the course of instruction.

Colonel Leo Melanson, the DAC and Deputy Commander, wrote the following which is an excerpt from the recommendation for the Meritorious Service Medal which I was awarded when I departed the Intelligence School for Panama: "After being highly successful as a first sergeant, Sergeant Major Carden was selected as the Intelligence School Secretariat Sergeant Major followed by appointment as the Sergeant Major, Directorate of Training and Doctrine. In both positions, his leadership abilities, technical competence and concern for soldiers were well known throughout the command.

In August 1988, Sergeant Major Carden was selected over nine senior sergeants major to be the Sergeant Major for the Deputy Assistant Commandant and Deputy Commander, U.S. Army Intelligence School, Fort Devens. He assumed responsibility for the technical supervision of all Signals Intelligence and Electronic

Warfare training conducted at the Intelligence School, Fort Devens, MA; the Intelligence Training Battalion, Goodfellow Air Force Base, TX; and the Intelligence Training Detachment, Pensacola, FL. His unparalleled knowledge of training and training development processes, sound analytical judgment and mature leadership style provided extraordinary continuity and stability through the tenures of two Deputy Commanders and two Commanders. He provided leadership and guidance to all school academic departments and directorates; corrected deficiencies in training and operations; and particularly noteworthy, over a two-year period, saved five per-cent of an annual population of 5,000 soldiers, sailors, airmen and Marines from failing their courses of instruction. His tenure was consistently characterized by relentless pursuit of excellence in the conduct of instruction, caring leadership and a genuine concern for the welfare of both students and permanent party personnel.

Sergeant Major Carden devoted the final year of his assignment at the Intelligence School to Department of Defense executive agent Morse Signals Intelligence training. He assumed responsibility for training that, since the 1950's, has historically had a 50 to 55 per-cent success rate. His implementation of positive student counseling, an innovative remedial training program, and treating trainees with dignity and respect directly contributed to a 91.3 per-cent success rate. He was pro-active in the classrooms of three academic divisions and garnered the respect and admiration of students, instructors and staff. His devotion to high quality instruction and positive leadership directly contributed to one of his instructors being selected as the U.S. Army Intelligence School Instructor of the Year."

THE MP

The Intelligence School Secretariat Sergeant Major was a position allocated to a Sergeant Major from the logistics field. Since Department of the Army didn't assign a logistics Sergeant Major to the Intelligence School, I had the job. My first few days on the job, I went around the directorate and met the other 219 people, both Military and civilian, that comprised the School Secretariat. One group that I met was the Military Police (MP) Section. Their Section Leader was Staff Sergeant Cicero Sastri. He was a spit and polish professional and the epitome of what people consider an MP to be like. His soldiers were strac... pressed and creased Battle Dress Uniforms (BDU) and highly shined bloused boots. You could place a newspaper next to any one of his MPs' boots and read it off the leather.

I sat down with Staff Sergeant Sastri to chit chat. I asked him if his records were in order for the upcoming Department of the Army promotion board and told him that I would be glad to help him prepare. He told me his career came to a screeching halt a few years earlier at his previous assignment and that there was no career progression in his future. His battalion commander, a lieutenant colonel, had administered an Article 15 (nonjudicial punishment) for failure to repair (late for work). A field grade Article 15 is definitely a career ender. He didn't have a snowball's chance in hell of ever overcoming this blemish on his record and nobody would buck the system to help him. I fault his First Sergeant and Sergeant Major for not stepping up to the plate. They allowed officers to threaten an NCO with a court martial and possibly lose everything for which he had devoted his life; or accept an Article 15 and be done with it. He was told that he had no right to appeal. His officer and NCO chain-of-command had lied to him.

I reviewed Staff Sergeant Sastri's microfiche and he had clearly been railroaded at his previous command. I considered the circumstances surrounding the charges against him just a little on the extenuating side. He was finishing a guard shift, and in a freak accident, a safe door was closed on his left index finger and it was severed at the first joint. He drove himself to the hospital. His chain-of-command stacked court martial charges against him for dereliction of duty and missing formation and if convicted, he was looking at being kicked out of the Army. He had just reenlisted prior to the accident and could retire with 20 years service if he accepted the nonjudicial punishment. He was caught between a rock and a hard spot and had everything to lose.

It took me nearly a month to get everything together that I needed. The packet that I was sure would exonerate him included the medical report regarding the incident, a legal opinion from the Fort Devens Judge Advocate General, and signatures of the Brigade Commander, Intelligence School Commander and the Fort Devens Commander. The packet was expedited to the Military Police Branch at Department of the Army. Staff Sergeant Sastri was cleared of all charges and his official file was corrected. The next order of business was to get his records before the Department of the Army promotion board. Staff Sergeant Sastri was selected for promotion to Sergeant First Class. I don't know if I really did him any favors because his next assignment was to the beautiful Pacific isle of Guam.

NCOA

The Non Commissioned Officers Association of the United States of America is a political and fraternal organization serving current and former enlisted personnel of the five branches of the American Armed Forces…Army, Navy, Air Force, Coast Guard and Marines. In 1985, I was signed up for a life membership by the Sergeant Major of the Army. In 1988, I was elected Chapter Chairman of the New England Chapter. I served in that capacity until late 1991 when I was reassigned from Fort Devens, Massachusetts to Corozal, Panama.

Rather than having a fraternal organization that consisted of mostly Senior NCOs at Fort Devens and a scattering of Air Force and Reserve Forces and National Guard Senior NCOs, I wanted to bring into our chapter young NCOs from all the services. I started by getting involved in the Fort Devens community.

Purely by luck, I met one of the brothers who owned a local supermarket chain. The DiGeronimo family owned the Victory Supermarket chain in several communities in Massachusetts and New Hampshire. I explained that I was trying to help the lower ranking families assigned at Fort Devens during the upcoming Thanksgiving Holiday. They donated 25 turkeys for Thanksgiving 1988. During the Thanksgiving holidays of 1989, 1990 and 1991 they donated another 25 turkeys for each holiday.

The week before Thanksgiving 1988, I picked up the turkeys and they were distributed to the First Sergeants who had requested them for their young married soldiers. During the Christmas holidays, those young soldiers on Fort Devens who didn't go home were given a Christmas party at the Enlisted Men's Club courtesy of the NCOA New England Chapter. Our membership was growing.

The week after Thanksgiving 1989, I was at a Sergeant Major meeting and the Post Sergeant Major said that there wouldn't be a Fort Devens Christmas Ball because the officers on post were bickering and nobody would take responsibility for it. Nobody said anything constructive, so I said that I would take charge of it as the NCOA Chapter Chairman and the ball would be strictly for enlisted soldiers and their guests. The Sergeant Major said that he had told the Post Commander that the Christmas Ball would happen and he was promised use of the

Community Club. The Sergeant Major also promised me use of a stage band from the Army Band. The ball was rolling.

To cover catering expenses from the club and to ensure maximum participation, ticket sales were set according to rank: $10.00 per individual and $20.00 per couple for young soldiers; $15.00 and $30.00 for mid-level NCOs; and $20.00 and $40.00 for Senior NCOs.

I formed a Joint-Service Color Guard with students from the Intelligence School and the Color Sergeant was a Marine Staff Sergeant. At the ball, the ceremonial portion and posting the Colors went flawlessly.

Soldiers who don't own or can't afford a formal dress uniform can wear their Class A uniform with a white shirt and black bowtie when attending a formal function. This ball was an opportunity for young soldiers and NCOs to learn about Military customs and heritage. It was also an opportunity for young spouses to have fun. Attendance was represented by all the Services.

The Army Band did an excellent job. I used their services a few more times over the next couple of years.

The 1989 Fort Devens Enlisted Christmas Ball was a total success. The Post Sergeant Major told me afterwards that some of the officers who didn't want to get involved with the original planning were offended that they couldn't attend. Oh well.

During the next two years, the New England Chapter was involved in the Military community providing assistance when needed. Our efforts were recognized by the NCOA national headquarters in San Antonio, Texas and I was personally awarded the Super Saxon Merit Award for the years 1989 and 1990.

THE STRANDED TRUCKER

Circa 1988. It was late summer, a class graduation day which meant it was Thursday, and it looked like I would be going to my home in Fitchburg a little early in the afternoon.

I decided to leave through the Verbeck Gate at Fort Devens and take a leisurely drive home on Route 2A. As I left the down town area of Ayer behind me, ahead of me was a tractor-trailer pulled over off the highway. As I passed the rig, the hood was up over the engine compartment and the driver was just jumping down to the ground from the bumper. He was covered in oil. I pulled over.

I asked the driver if he needed any help and he thanked me for stopping. His truck had broken down, he had called his company, and they were sending a tow truck. It was a bad day.

This was supposed to be a one day trip. He was from Missouri, had dropped off a tractor-trailer in Framingham and was asked to deliver another tractor-trailer to Shirley. He almost made it. Now he was stuck in a small town. No money to speak of, no credit cards and no clean clothes. He had a plane ticket to fly back to Missouri the next day.

I told him to hop in my car and we'd take care of the clothes situation. I drove back to the down town area of Ayer to the western wear store at the intersection of Route 2A and Main Street. I bought him a shirt, blue jeans and under garments and put the items on my credit card. Then I went to the bank next door, got some cash, and handed him one hundred dollars. Next, I got him a motel room in Ayer and wished him a good trip home.

Over his protestations, I told him that my Father is a truck driver and if he were ever in a similar situation, I would hope someone would help him.

Before and during the Gulf War, I was assigned at the U.S. Army Intelligence School, Fort Devens, Massachusetts. We provided critical intelligence skills training to soldiers scheduled for deployment and also training to Kuwaiti soldiers, princes and sheiks. We taught them how to survive in a chemical and biological environment.

In addition, I represented the Commander, Fort Devens in New England communities to answer questions and help to dispel their fears regarding their loved ones who were about to be deployed or were already deployed.

Just before Desert Storm, my Career Manager at Department of the Army called me on a Thursday afternoon and asked if I could be ready Monday morning to deploy to Saudi Arabia to take over a Military Intelligence Battalion. I told him of course, and on Friday and early Saturday I completed all my inoculations, got my personal affairs in order and updated my Survivor Benefit Plan. I also dusted off my Survivor Packet left over from when I had a Special Forces Battalion. I was ready to go.

I called my Career Manager back Monday morning for additional instructions and he told me to stand down. They had someone already in-country who had just been promoted and they were going to give him a shot.

I went back to the public relations stuff I was doing for the Army. I wound up getting some descent press coverage considering the part of the country I was in and the abundance of liberal press that wasn't too keen on the Military.

THE NIGHT BEFORE DESERT STORM

Circa January 16th, 1991. The United States Army Intelligence School Devens (USAISD) was relatively quiet at night except for ongoing specialized computer-based Morse code training for three classrooms of 30 students in the Morse Collection Department (MCD). This evening's classes had started at 9:00 pm and I was evaluating the conduct of instruction around 11:00 pm. In each classroom the students were asking their instructors about the impending war with Iraq. They were concerned because Saddam Hussein had ignored the United Nations edict to withdraw from Kuwait. These were young soldiers, sailors, airmen and Marines who, for the most part, had friends and immediate family members deployed on Desert Shield. There were mothers and fathers, brothers and sisters, aunts and uncles, cousins and maybe even some grand parents who were deployed. There wasn't a whole lot of learning going on.

I told all the instructors to give their students a ten minute break and then to bring them to the Command Conference Room. Since Desert Shield started, I had been representing the U.S. Army in New England communities to give them the U.S. position on why we were doing what we were doing and to soothe their fears regarding loved ones who had been or would be deployed. My students were about to receive the same presentation.

After twenty minutes, I said: "O.K. guys, bottom line. We have the best fighting force in the world. We have the best people, the best training and best equipment. The NBC suit (Nuclear, Biological, Chemical) is the best and will do its job. No pissant dictator is going to push around the United States of America."

And then I said: "If I were the President for one day, this is what I would do. I would go on prime time TV at nine o'clock at night and I would say: My fellow Americans, as I speak, the United States Air Force is bombing the hell out of Baghdad. Saddam Hussein started this war and we will damn well finish it!"

The following night, President Bush went on prime time TV and he said: "My fellow Americans, as I speak...."

My job in Panama, 1991-1993, was performing duty as the Operations Sergeant Major for the Military Intelligence Brigade that supported the United States Army Southern Command. I had a million dollar annual budget; kept tabs on on-going operations in the areas of counter-insurgency and counter-drug in Central and South America; and I was the tasking authority responsible for security of the Panama Canal. My area of operation included Central and South America and the coastal waters of the Atlantic and Pacific Oceans. Brigade assets included 300 agents, five ships and fourteen aircraft. Occasionally, I took a trip to Cancun, Mexico and Tegucigalpa, Honduras.

The first year of my assignment was relatively uneventful. Insurgents were ineffective, we were doing our job regarding the drug trade, and the Canal remained secure. Leisure time, when I had any, was spent on the white sand beach or playing blackjack in the casino at the El Panama Hotel.

The second year, I was kept quite busy. Hurricane Andrew created a logistics nightmare. I directed all the planes to Louisiana and Georgia. The ships were scattered to the four winds and I had to find safe havens for them. One hid behind Cuba, three headed for Louisiana and one rode out the storm. After the hurricane, all the ships and planes returned safely to Panama. A drug mission culminated with a barge containing twenty tons of cocaine being interdicted off the coast of Peru. Insurgents stepped up efforts to thwart President Bush's trip to Panama. They attempted drive-by shootings at U.S. facilities and a last ditch effort to disrupt the visit was to ambush and kill two young American soldiers on the Pan-American Highway. An office was established with the Panamanian National Police to develop leads and track down the perpetrators. It was determined who planned and implemented the murders and a $200,000.00 reward was established to pay for information leading to his capture. The leader of the insurgents, the son of a Panamanian politician, was never captured and he went on to become prominent in future Panamanian politics.

President Bush's visit was uneventful.

A Battalion Command Sergeant Major had to return to the

States for a family emergency. Department of the Army didn't have a replacement, so I was also dual-hated to fill the position.

I served two years in Panama and went to Fort Bragg, North Carolina for my final two years of active duty. I started my career as a Private First Class with Special Forces and my swan song was a final assignment, culminating 30 years, as a Sergeant Major with the United States Army Special Operations Command.

Army officers become officers through various ways. First, and probably most prestigious, is the Military Academy at West Point, New York. Then there is the Reserve Officer Training Corps (ROTC) offered at college campuses. For active duty soldiers, there is Officer Candidate School (OCS). And another way is through direct appointment which some people call a battlefield commission. General officers of the 1960s and 1970s became general officers for the most part because they were either graduates of West Point or they were exceptional products of OCS. General officers of the 1980s, 1990s and this century are a product of their own abilities, not how they came to become officers. Every general officer will tell you that he owes his success in large part to a squad leader or a platoon sergeant who took him under his wing when he was a young lieutenant. Lieutenants who wouldn't listen to their NCOs became captains who wouldn't listen or take advice also. They didn't progress much beyond captain.

There is only a hand full of captains that I knew during my 30-year career that I truly respected and would follow into hell. They are: Paul Menoher who retired as a lieutenant general, Wayne Stone who retired as a colonel and was one of my commanders, C.J. McKee who retired as a lieutenant colonel and was also one of my commanders, and Dean Shultz who was an Air Force weather officer that I worked with at Fort Bragg. He was promoted to major shortly before I retired. Then there was John Watkins. He was a Department of the Army civilian when I knew him and he was my rater. John had been an Army captain and paratrooper who was medically retired after a very serious parachuting injury. The two years I knew him at Fort Bragg, he was a good colleague and friend.

And last, but certainly not least, was Anthony G. Kaliher. Captain Tony Kaliher and I worked together leading and teaching new soldiers in a training company. He was an exceptional leader and somewhat of a skeptic. Sometimes his skepticism led us into murky waters. One afternoon I received a phone call from the battalion commander and he asked me to come to his office. When I arrived, he asked me what my job was. I wasn't quite sure where this was going, but I told him my job was to lead and train; and to ensure the welfare and morale of my soldiers. Lieutenant Colonel Thomas Hanlon, one of the finest officers I have ever met, looked me in the eye and said, "First Sergeant, your primary job is to keep your captain out of trouble. Take this note he sent me this morning and give it back to him. And I'm quite sure if the brigade commander wants his advice, he'll ask for it." Captain Kaliher and I had adjoining offices. When I returned to my office, I went into his. He was sitting at his desk and smiling sheepishly. We discussed his note and I told him that in the future we needed to screen our, meaning his, correspondence before it was sent forward. By the way, we had the best cadre and best company in the training brigade.

Most paratroopers have jump stories. Since I was on jump status most of my 30 year career, I have a few myself. Recorded here are some that came to mind.

Circa 1969. Can Tho, South Vietnam. Several of us had an administrative jump from a helicopter with our Vietnamese counterparts, the Luc Luong Dac Biet (Vietnamese Special Forces). When my canopy opened, I was showered with dirt, leaves and twigs. Whoever used that parachute before must have landed in trees.

Circa 1971. Turner Drop Zone, Fort Devens. Temperature was 20 degrees with a wind chill below zero. Helicopter jump from 1,200 feet. I landed in the creek that flows through the drop zone. I broke through the ice. The wind was gusting 20 knots and filled my canopy. My harness quick release was frozen shut from packed snow, mud and ice. I was along for one hell of a ride. Other jumpers tried to collapse the chute; some couldn't get a grasp, others were knocked down. The wind was blowing one way; the creek took a turn in another direction. At the bend in the creek was a huge boulder. The canopy went over the boulder and kept going. I was right behind it. There is a reason that a military helmet is referred to as a brain bucket. One of my two best friends, Staff Sergeant James A. Smith III (Jim Smith), got a grip on the edge of the canopy and threw his 200-plus pound body onto it, collapsing the canopy. My forward motion, or from where I was, my backward motion, halted about two feet from the boulder.

Circa 1972. Boise, Idaho in July. We flew in a C-130 Combat Talon aircraft from Fort Devens, Massachusetts to Boise, Idaho. In the early afternoon, we jumped from about 1000 feet into an open field across the street from the National Guard Armory. Nothing really significant about the jump other than the people on the ground were waiting for us with a big galvanized steel garbage can filled with ice and Coors beer.

Circa 1973. Yomitan Drop Zone, Okinawa. My first jump on Okinawa. My friends had told me that the ground was hard as concrete and if at all possible, head for the grassy areas. I heeded their advice. When my feet hit the grass, I was still falling. I had landed in elephant grass inside a large depression. My canopy spread out on top of the grass about three feet above me. Then it was a matter of making my way through the grass and climbing out of the hole. My laughing friends were awaiting my arrival.

Circa 1975. Jumpmaster School. An Army Jumpmaster is responsible for the lives of the jumpers in his charge. On one of our numerous practice Jumpmaster jumps, a fellow classmate was performing the safety check of the aircraft door and fuselage. The safety check requires grasping the side edges of the doorway and leaning outside the aircraft to check for sharp edges and any safety hazards. He fell out of the airplane.

Circa 1975. Fort Hood, Texas. We flew from Fort Devens, Massachusetts to somewhere in the desert at Fort Hood. We arrived over our drop zone at 2:00 am and jumped into a dark night sky with no moon or stars. Our drop altitude was supposed to be 1,250 feet, but we were actually dropped from 2,000 feet. Night vision was zero and you couldn't make out an outline of the horizon. So in a situation like that, you judge your rate of descent and the time you're in the air, and prepare to execute a parachute landing fall. Guessing that you're about 100 feet above the ground, you release your 120 pounds of equipment that is secured to your parachute harness by a 10-foot tether, and you wait to hit the ground. And you wait, and wait, and wait and start talking to yourself. You don't know that you've been dropped from an altitude 800 feet higher than what you were supposed to be. Your equipment starts oscillating below you. Not a good sign because this causes you to sway forward and backward. If your feet don't hit the ground first, it's going to be a bad day at Black Rock. Your sense of hearing is keen. What you hear isn't comforting. Exclamations of pain. At least you know you're close to the ground and awaiting the inevitable. In mid swing, my feet hit the ground and I believe I executed one of the most perfect parachute landing falls I have ever done. I hit my quick release and got out of my harness. Exhilaration was the feeling. I took about three steps and walked into a cactus. One of those cactuses that stands ten feet tall and has arms that point up in the air. The sounds of pain I heard earlier were paratroopers crashing into cacti. The next two weeks were spent removing cactus thorns.

Circa 1976. In a six month period, I parachuted five times and had five parachute malfunctions in a row. The malfunctions mainly consisted of torn canopies or panels that were shredded. The first four jumps I rode in to the ground. The fifth jump, I deployed my reserve parachute because my canopy looked like it had been packed by Freddie Kruger.

Circa 1977. Normandy Drop Zone, Fort Bragg. Altitude for this jump was 2,500 feet. People were descending all around me and I was staying in one place. I was caught in an air pocket. I tried spilling air from my canopy and at one point even tried to collapse my parachute. Whatever direction the air pocket was going, I was along for the ride. The air pocket carried me two miles to the Cross Creek Mall just outside of Fort Bragg. That's where I broke free. Right over the 401 bypass, a four-lane highway. I steered away from the highway and landed in the wooded area across the street from the mall.

Circa 1980. Bad Toelz, Germany. An administrative jump from a helicopter. There was a light mist and the air was heavy which created a very slow descent. Our drop zone was a cow pasture and as we were descending, the German farmer was moving his cattle off the field. I landed on a nice fresh cow chip and slid along my side through it.

The final jump story isn't about me, but about my friend Jose. He lost a leg the previous year when he hit high tension lines. So whenever he was scheduled for a jump, he carried along his jumping leg. When we were issued parachutes, he would sit down and take off his walking leg and put on his jumping leg. He would secure his leg to his harness, and after he landed, he would switch legs. Jose also had a running leg for when he wanted to leave us in his dust.

My Swan Song

My career in Special Forces started as a young Private First Class. My first assignment was to a new elite unit designated as a Special Operations Detachment and I was a member of a Special Operations Team A. My career was ending with the rank of Sergeant Major in the duty position of Senior Intelligence Advisor to the Chief of the Intelligence Support Division in the Office of the Deputy Chief of Staff for Intelligence at the United States Army Special Operations Command.

My first major undertaking was heading the Military Intelligence Relook Task Force. Based on my expertise and numerous years of experience in Military Intelligence support to Special Operations, I was selected to interview Special Forces Group Commanders, S-2 (Intelligence) and S-3 (Operations) Officers. Endemic problems were blatantly staring me in the face, so I expanded my interviews to include Commanders of Operational Detachments A (ODA), Team Sergeants and Intelligence Sergeants. I also interviewed the Special Forces Group Military Intelligence Detachment leadership down to the Special Operations Team A (SOTA) team members.

My office may have been at Fort Bragg, North Carolina, but I was becoming a world traveler. The Air Force Staff Weather Officer was somewhat of a jokester and he placed a map on the wall of the Operations Center with push pins in it to denote my location at his daily weather briefings. He tagged me with the nickname "Waldo" as in "Where in the world is Waldo?"

My travels took me to United States Army Special Forces Command (USAFC), United States Army Civil Affairs & Psychological Operations Command (USACAPOC), Security Assistance Training Management Office (SATMO), 160th Special Operations Aviation Regiment (160th SOAR), and the 75th Ranger Regiment. I had worked with all of the aforementioned commands in the past and could associate with them and understand their Intelligence requirements.

The results of my interviews combined with those of the team tasked to obtain results from research and development helped to determine the best Military Intelligence support required for Special Operations through the year 2020. On November 30th, 1994 I received an impact award of the Army Commendation Medal (ARCOM). The results of the Task Force have become evident during the past eight years in this time of war.

In my day job, I was responsible for USASOC intelligence training, Readiness Training (REDTRAIN) and Live Environment Training (LET). I conducted coordination with Intelligence and Security Command (INSCOM) and the Intelligence School at Fort Huachuca, Arizona for delivery of the Tactical Voice Intercept Trainer to the 3rd and 7th Special Forces Groups at Fort Bragg. I actively sought intelligence training opportunities for USASOC MI soldiers and personally coordinated with United States Special Operations Command (USSOC), Defense Intelligence Agency (DIA) and world-wide military intelligence units. I managed a $650,000.00 intelligence training budget and negotiated an additional $250,000.00 from the Pentagon. I established and maintained close liaison with the Deputy Chief of Staff for Resource Management (DSCRM) and major subordinate commands to ensure proper funding and conduct of quality training for Special Forces MI soldiers. The REDTRAIN Program I had set up for Special Forces in 1979 was just as viable in the 1990s. The USASOC regulation governing REDTRAIN was verbatim what I had written for the 5th Special Forces Group. One thing about the Military, regulation writers have literary license to borrow, sometimes verbatim, from other works.

I knew exactly where to go when I went to the Pentagon to negotiate for more REDTRAIN funding for Special Forces. Nothing had changed since 1979. And, it was Dejavu. Only this time, a lieutenant colonel was responsible for disbursing funds to major commands. I showed him how the money would be used and how travel expenses would be cut. He approved my request and I had an additional $225,000.00.

Since I was in the building, I stopped by the office of the Deputy Chief of Staff for Intelligence. I was met by a Sergeant First Class in an outer office and she informed General Menoher that I was waiting to see him. He told her to send me in. I entered an ante room and saw the General's door to my right and headed toward it. There must have been ten Colonels with brief cases sitting in chairs along the outer walls waiting for an audience with the General. General Menoher was sitting at his desk and came to meet me at the entrance to his office. I congratulated him on being selected for a third star and we talked about things in general for a few minutes. Then I extended an invitation to him for my retirement ceremony that was scheduled for April 28th, 1995. He told me that as long as there weren't any pressing issues, he would make every effort to be there.

My return flight to Fort Bragg was scheduled for the following day, so I drove to Fort Belvoir, Virginia to meet my old friend Art Johnson. He had been a Marine in his younger days, saw the light, and reenlisted in the Army. Art Johnson was now the Command Sergeant Major, United States Army Intelligence and Security Command (INSCOM). Art and I discussed career progression for Army Special Operations Forces (ARSOF) soldiers and my recommendations coming out of the MI Relook Task Force. He told me that he was really glad that I was the person who ran the show. There was a whole lot of interest at INSCOM and at Department of the Army on how it would affect the future of intelligence support to Special Operations.

Legion of Merit
Soldier's Medal
Bronze Star Medal-2 awards
Meritorious Service Medal-4 awards
Air Medal
Army Commendation Medal-4 awards
Army Achievement Medal-2awards
Good Conduct Medal-10th award
National Defense Service Medal-2 awards
Vietnam Service Medal w/9 campaign stars
Armed Forces Expeditionary Medal
NCO Professional Development Ribbon w/numeral 4
Army Service Ribbon
Overseas Service Ribbon w/numeral 3
Vietnam Campaign Ribbon w/device 60

Presidential Unit Citation (Army-Air Force)
Meritorious Unit Commendation-3 awards
Navy Meritorious Unit Commendation
Air Force Outstanding Unit Award
Republic of Vietnam Gallantry Cross Unit Citation w/Palm
Republic of Vietnam Civil Actions Medal Unit Citation

Combat Infantryman Badge (CIB)
Special Forces Tab
Aircraft Crewmember Badge
Master Parachutist Badge
Republic of Vietnam Parachutist Badge
Imperial Iranian Parachutist Badge
Military Intelligence Corps Distinctive Unit Insignia

Expert Weapon Qualification Badge
  -M16 Rifle
  -9mm Pistol
  -.45 Caliber Pistol

JUN65-FEB66

Basic Combat Training, Advanced Individual Training, and Basic Airborne Training

MAR66-AUG66

403rd Special Operations Detachment
3rd Special Forces Group, Fort Bragg, North Carolina

SEP66-FEB70

403rd Special Operations Detachment
5th Special Forces Group, Republic of Vietnam

MAR70-JUL72

402nd Special Operations Detachment
10th Special Forces Group, Fort Devens, Massachusetts

AUG72-AUG73

7th Radio Research Field Station, Udorn, Thailand

SEP73-MAY74

400th Special Operations Detachment
1st Special Forces Group, Camp Chinen, Okinawa

JUN74-JUL74

400th Special Operations Detachment
US Army John F. Kennedy Center for Military Assistance
Fort Bragg, North Carolina

AUG74-AUG81

5th Special Forces Group, Fort Bragg, North Carolina
　　400th Special Operations Detachment
　　14th Combat Tactical Intelligence Company
　　5th Group Military Intelligence Company
　　Military Intelligence Company (Group)

SEP81-APR83
> 331st Army Security Agency Company
(Operations) (Forward), V Corps, Karlsruhe, Germany

MAY83-JUL84
> 330th Electronic Warfare Aviation Company
> 2nd Aerial Exploitation Battalion, VII Corps
> Kaiserslautern, Germany

AUG84-JUL85
> Support Battalion, 10th Special Forces Group
> Fort Devens, Massachusetts

AUG85-DEC86
> B Company, 1st Battalion, 2nd School Brigade
> Fort Devens, Massachusetts

JAN87-DEC91
> US Army Intelligence School, Fort Devens, Massachusetts
>> Sergeant Major, School Secretariat
>> Sergeant Major, Deputy Assistant Commandant
>>> -Directorate of Training
>>>   and Doctrine
>>> -Electronic Warfare Department
>>> -Morse Collection Department

JAN92-DEC93
> Headquarters, 470th Military Intelligence Brigade
> Corozal, Republic of Panama

JAN94-APR95
> Intelligence Support Division
> Office of the Deputy Chief of Staff for Intelligence
> US Army Special Operations Command, Fort Bragg, NC

I received a phone call from the Deputy Chief of Staff for Intelligence (DCSINT), United States Army Special Operations Command (USASOC) and he asked me if I could stop by his office. When I arrived, he said that the planning had to begin for my retirement ceremony. I told him that I really didn't want a ceremony. There were many formations that I stood in on cold days and hot days for retirement ceremonies of people I never knew. Granted, it was tradition to honor service to our country, but I didn't want to put people through the same things I had gone through. As far as I was concerned, a simple get together in the conference room with associates at 10:00 am on a Friday morning would be fine with me. Then afterwards, people who didn't have a whole lot to do could take the rest of the day off and enjoy a long weekend.

John Watkins, my boss and friend, was tasked with making the arrangements. Nothing was laid in concrete, yet. He shot gunned a message out to the world with an announcement and waited for responses. After about a week, John stopped by my office and told me that he had received numerous messages from people who would attend and the conference room wasn't going to cut it. It was his way of telling me that I wasn't going to have my way.

In the interim, Lieutenant General Paul Menoher, the Deputy Chief of Staff for Intelligence, United States Army, sent me his regrets in a hand-written note that he would be unable to attend my retirement ceremony.

John was doing a great job adhering to what I wanted. He booked the Command Auditorium so people could sit and not have to stand for any length of time. Also, I didn't want a speaker. I just wanted to walk across the stage, be presented my retirement papers, say a few words to the people who came, and walk off the stage. Reception in the hallway to follow.

At exactly 10:00 am on a Friday morning, the Army Band struck the first note and I marched from the back of the Auditorium to center stage. The National Anthem was played. I sat down along with the full auditorium. I think maybe people passing by thought there might be a movie, so they entered the auditorium to check it out. Nobody was required to be there. I saw some faces in the audience that I hadn't seen in years.

John Watkins performed as a master of ceremonies. He told the audience what I had requested and that after the ceremony there would be a reception in the hallway and people who didn't have to go back to work could enjoy a long weekend. Also, there wouldn't be a formal speaker. He acknowledged the people in the audience by stating that they all volunteered to attend. And on that note, he said although I didn't want a drawn out ceremony, there were some things about my 30-year career that they should hear. His remarks received a standing ovation. I was somewhat embarrassed, but proud.

Then John read the citation and the Commander presented me with a Legion of Merit and my retirement orders. A reception followed in the hallway.

BOOK 3

Book 3

It's Over

The active duty Military chapter of my life officially ended on July 1st, 1995. Shortly after that, another chapter ended. Gracemary and I were no longer together. Regardless of the reasons, it was over, and we each went on to new horizons.

I had four greatest days in my life. Each one was when I was in the delivery room for each of my children. I missed a lot of birthdays, holidays and special events; but I was present each time they drew their first breath. Their Mother was the primary person who taught them their value systems. Gracemary also taught them how to be self sufficient and how to do electrical work, plumbing and common sense stuff; and most importantly, respect for others.

Every parent has a favorite memory of an event that stands out regarding their children. These are my memories of such events for Matthew, Steven, Dominic and Catherine.

Two years after I retired, when I was the big 5-0, I took them to lunch at a small family restaurant. After we finished with lunch, the waitress brought the check and offered me the senior citizen discount. My grown children thought it was very funny.

When Dominic was six years old, we placed him in a music program. His instrument was the Alto Sax. He didn't want to do it. His brothers told him practice hard because when he got older the girls love boys who play the saxophone. He practiced hard. He constantly practiced. Dominic went on to play in the high school marching band and the stage band.

Steven was a cross country runner. He had a state ranking. He was leading a race when he stepped in a pot hole and broke a growth plate in his foot. He still finished second in that race. His cross country days were over. His coach tried him out in hurdles. Steven was a natural.

Matthew was a mediocre pole vaulter in high school. I say this with the utmost respect for his pole vaulting abilities. When he went to the University of Massachusetts at Amherst, Matthew was their star pole vaulter.

When Catherine was six years old and Dominic was eight, she was walking home from school with her girl friends when she saw the school bully sitting on Dominic and pummeling him. Catherine dropped her school books and ran toward him yelling, "You leave my brother alone!" She charged into him hitting him in the chest and knocking him over. She started pounding on him with her little six year old fists. The kid never bothered Dominic again.

Catherine and Dominic were in the marching band. Catherine was a flag bearer and the girls had a flag drill routine. Catherine and I were having a Dad-Daughter talk when she said to me, "Dad, my boyfriend is gay." I was thinking he damned well better be. I asked her how she felt about that and she told me he was fun to be around and there were more important things to be concerned about. After one of her practice sessions, Catherine asked me if I could drop the kids off at their homes. Everybody got in the car and I followed directions to each of their homes. When I dropped off the last girl, I asked Catherine who she was. She said, "Dad that was my boyfriend!"

My proudest day involving Catherine was attending her graduation from Nursing School.

Matt and Steve were as close to one another as my brother Mike and I were. When I walked into the house one day after work, Gracemary told me to go get my boys. I knew there was something up when she called them "your boys." Above the City of Fitchburg, Massachusetts is seven-eighths of a huge boulder on the side of a hill that over looks the city. The other eighth of the boulder sits at the end of Boulder Avenue in downtown Fitchburg. I went to the top of the hill. Two of my rappelling ropes were tied off at the top and Matt and Steve were on the other ends. They were continuing a time-honored tradition and painting Matt's high school graduation year on the boulder. I instructed them to come up, it was time for supper. They did a good job.

Another time I walked through the door and Gracemary said, "Go get your son." This time Matt was in Fitchburg at the Army recruiter's office. The next day the recruiter called Matt and asked him why he hadn't mentioned that his dad was a Sergeant Major. Matt said, "You didn't ask."

POLITICS AND ME

Politics as a vocation was nearly a reality for me. The Mayor of Fremont, Nebraska was also the President of the Chamber of Commerce and I had a part-time job at the Chamber of Commerce from the age of 13 to the age of 18. Dwight Collins was a good mayor and I was impressed with how he ran the city. I was bitten by the political bug and wanted to be a mayor. But my destiny was to be a soldier. My whole adult life, I never missed voting in a national election.

In 1985, I met a middle-age man handing out flyers outside a grocery store. He was a candidate for the Office of Mayor in the city of Fitchburg, Massachusetts. His name was Jeff Bean. Assisting him was his wife and about six or seven of their children. What really impressed me about Jeff and his wife was that they had been foster parents for many years. They adopted troubled children and gave them a good home. They also ensured that each of their children received a college education after they graduated from high school. Although I wasn't associated with his political affiliation, I supported him. I helped him on weekends holding placards and I also helped to get out the vote on Election Day. I was one of the original members of the "Bean Machine."

Jeff became a good friend and he also won the election. He won a few more after that too. Periodically, I would receive a phone call from Jeff asking me to attend a political function for an up and coming politician. When I was promoted to Sergeant Major, Jeff presented me with a certificate proclaiming me as Honorary Mayor for a day. Of course, the day had already passed.

After I retired, Jeff called me and asked if I would represent the city on a board of directors to help low-income families. I told him that I would be glad to help. So, I was the official representative of the City of Fitchburg on the Board of Directors for the Montachusett Opportunity Council (MOC). I performed this voluntary public service for five years. In 2000, Jeff was appointed to a position with FEMA, an appointment that crossed party lines. I decided to end my sojourn into politics.

MY BROTHER JOE

This story is about my brother Joe. He was my parents' fourth child of seven and was named Joseph Lynn Carden. I'm writing this story because I doubt if any one else ever will. If ever there were a person born on this planet whose whole life would be heartache and pain, it was Joe. He had the same love and nurturing that his brothers and sisters had growing up and his life was miserable. Joe was nearly 40 years old when he died a year before I retired in 1995.

Joe was a talented charcoal artist and musician when he was a young lad. He got caught up in the hard drug subculture of the 1970s and the demons followed him the rest of his life. Joe was a smart and talented guy, but he never wanted responsibility. When he was in his mid-twenties, Joe joined the Salvation Army and put his musical talents to use. He was even appointed as a captain. Whenever there was a chance of him becoming successful, Joe walked away from the success.

Joe traveled to Alaska and got a job as a line cook on the Alaska pipeline. He was there a few years and then moved south to work as a cook on the oil derricks in the Gulf of Mexico. Joe eventually became a master chef and worked in a five-star hotel in New Orleans, Louisiana. Then one day, Joe walked away and moved to Denver, Colorado.

Joe played the guitar and performed daily as a sidewalk musician. He survived on pocket change. My parents had tried numerous times through the years to contact him, but he would always move on. I always knew where he was and informed my parents because he didn't keep in touch. Because of my line of work and a security clearance with a string of caveats, the FBI kept tabs on me, my associates and my family.

In 1994, shortly before his fortieth birthday, Joe went to my parents' home and he died in the room they had prepared for him. Joe had AIDS.

Spring 1995. For her birthday, I bought Gracemary a candy apple red Chrysler LHS with a light gray leather interior and bucket seats. For my retirement and what I thought would be the last new car I would ever buy, I bought a gun metal gray Lincoln with a light gray leather interior and a split-bench front seat. Although the Lincoln was an extremely comfortable ride; for me at least, leather wasn't everything it was made out to be. Hot in the summer and cold in the winter. So the following year, I bought a Ford Crown Victoria with a cloth split-bench seat.

Spring 2000. The Crown Vic served me well, but it was time for a change. Next up was a Dodge Intrepid ES "C" package that included a cloth split-bench front seat. Light gray exterior and dark gray interior. This car was as comfortable as my Lincoln.

Spring 2006. With a growing family, Dominic, my number three son, needed a bigger car than the compact car he was driving. So I gave him my mint condition Intrepid. Since I live in New England, a four-wheel drive vehicle should serve me well. I have acquired an appreciation for good quality older things, so I made my decision on buying a 1999 Dodge Ram 4x4 extended cab. Just one minor glitch. The truck wouldn't start in fog, snow or rain. The problem was humidity, but my mechanic couldn't find the source and it never seemed to rain whenever I would drop the truck off for maintenance. The truck not occasionally starting was useful for giving people directions to my house. I would just tell them to look for the gray house with the green truck in the driveway that never starts in the rain. Exactly one year ago, the catalytic converter was replaced.

Spring 2009. The new catalytic converter, still under warranty, sounded like a can of marbles and smelled like rotten eggs. I turned the truck in for another new catalytic converter, an oil change, and a tune up. It was raining when I left the truck at the garage. It sat for four days in the rain awaiting the parts. When the catalytic converter arrived, it took him a day to get the truck started. Oh, really? The catalytic converter was replaced. It took him another day to find the source of the arcing electrical thing that for years caused the truck not to start in the rain. And the oil change and tune up were completed. I went to the garage to pick up my truck that never starts in the rain. It was pouring down rain and the truck had been parked outside all day. My mechanic, standing in the rain next to the truck, handed me the key as I climbed inside and got comfortable behind the steering wheel. I didn't touch the accelerator and I put the key in the ignition. I turned the key. The truck purred like a kitten. My mechanic had a beaming smile as he gave me a thumbs up.

Circa December 1995. Auto sales was the vocation I chose after retiring. I really wasn't impressed with the professionalism, or lack thereof, I encountered when interviewing for managerial positions in the business world. I actually walked out of my last interview because I was told I had to do something. I said, "No I don't." My whole life was based on respect for others and I didn't see it happening with some so-called reputable corporations.

After three months in new car sales, I was elected Union Steward. This position was normally never considered for anyone with less than eighteen months experience in the business. This happened just before contract negotiations and I negotiated a new and better salary plus commission structure for sales personnel. Additionally, I achieved Chrysler Corporation Gold Certification for customer satisfaction. The certification structure is Bronze, Silver and Gold. Along with an engraved plaque and certificate, I was also presented a gold ring.

A few weeks before Christmas, shortly after opening, a young woman and her daughter walked into the showroom. The woman's name was Amy and her daughter's name was Susan. Little Susan was five years old. They were on a quest to find a new family vehicle. The men in the family, Bruce Senior and Bruce Junior., were at home getting ready for football watching. That was their job for the day. I told the two women of the family that I would be glad to help them in their quest. The next couple of hours were spent trying out a few new cars that would be suitable for and benefit their family. During the time I was showing cars to them, Susan referred to me as "The Car Man."

Amy thanked me for spending time with her and her daughter and I told her that I was glad to provide the information she needed. She was off to continue her quest. After they left, I wrote a thank you card and placed it in the out-going mail. A few days later, Amy and Susan returned to the showroom. Bruce Junior was with them. Amy thanked me for the card and told me that Susan wanted to see The Car Man. Their quest was nearly complete and Bruce Senior was the decision maker.

The next few days I was in and out of the showroom. The union was taking up some time and I was transferring a couple of vehicles with a dealership in Connecticut. When I made my final trip to Connecticut and returned to my dealership, there was a pastry dish waiting for me on my desk. The receptionist told me that a lady and her little daughter had dropped it off earlier in the day. There was a Christmas card with the pastries and it was addressed to "The Car Man."

I never saw them again…until recently. Fourteen years had passed when Amy and Susan approached me. I recognized Amy immediately and Susan was no longer the little five-year-old. She had grown into a lovely young lady. We talked about the car quest fourteen years earlier. Amy regretted not buying a car from me and I told her that Bruce made the decision that he felt was right for his family. As we were going our separate ways, Susan smiled and said, "Good bye, Car Man."

Valentine's Day 1999. Mary Linda Baker was shopping for a new vehicle for her craft making business. Her son, Brian was with her. She was looking at minivans and needed a reliable vehicle that she could use for storage and also transporting her product. Her selection was a new Dodge Grand Caravan. She was a savvy buyer, didn't want any additional frills, and was paying cash. The paperwork and bill of sale were all in order, her insurance was verified, and I started the process for her vehicle registration.

The following day, they returned to the showroom. Brian wanted a new truck. The same process as the day before was repeated, only this time with Brian. When Brian and I were alone doing paperwork, he said, "Why don't you ask my Mom out?" His question caught me by surprise, but I agreed to do it. So, scheduling conflicts aside, Mary Linda and I had dinner in a small family restaurant one month later. During the summer, I helped Mary Linda and her Mother at a couple of local craft fairs. This was also when I decided to leave auto sales and went back into retirement.

Circa Fall 1999. Mary Linda and I bought a house. It had to be big enough to store product (a garage and storage shed also helped in that area), and it eventually had to provide shelter for us, ten cats, four birds and a dog. We also started private ballroom dance lessons. Mary Linda wanted to dance at her son's wedding. So now I was a retired Special Forces Sergeant Major, making little stuffed animals and ballroom dancing.

New Year 2000. We had a table on the dance floor at a Worcester four star hotel. Catered dinner and dancing. Tango, Foxtrot, Swing and Latin dances. It was a fun night. In the spring, we danced a Tango that was showcased on local cable television. In the summer, Brian got married. Mary Linda danced at her son's wedding.

THE FROG LADY

In 1999 when I met Mary Linda Baker, she worked in the plastics industry. She was the buyer for an injection molding company. Throughout the years, her company had been bought, sold and reorganized numerous times. Her company reorganized and down-sized twice during 2001. In late December, the company closed its doors for the annual one-week Christmas shut-down. Mary Linda returned to work at the beginning of the New Year, and at the end of her first day back at work; she was out of a job. Twenty-eight years of her life ended at the stroke of 5:00 pm on January 2, 2002.

Mary Linda was no longer encumbered by an eight to five job and could devote all of her time to her enterprise: craft making. She makes bean bags. Specifically: frogs. Children and adults say her frogs look like "Elmo;" but they were around long before Elmo came on the scene. In addition to frogs, Mary Linda also makes snakes, lizards and turtles. Her bean bags are filled with polymer beads. There is no odor, and if they get wet, they just need to be air dried. No more going to a day job and then working on her crafts five or six hours a night. She could now devote all of her time to craft making.

Mary Linda is talented and also makes pinecone wreaths. The wreaths encompass collecting the various types of pinecones in all types of weather and temperatures throughout the year. She collects the pinecones, bakes them to bring out sap and kill spiders and bugs, cleans them, soaks them, and then dries them. She collects acorns from the tree overlooking her Mother's gravesite, bakes them, removes the caps and drills a hole in them, and feeds the nuts to the squirrels and chipmunks in our back yard. She sizes the pinecones and secures them to wire frames that are between eight and twenty-four inches in diameter. The pinecones and acorn caps are hand-wired into the frame. There is no glue in her wreaths. A large finished wreath could easily have a thirty inch diameter; be made with a half dozen different types of pinecones; and be adorned with over 200 acorn caps. Mary Linda created the pinecone wreath that hangs in our living room nearly 30 years ago.

Mary Linda has been making her bean bags for almost 30 years. Initially, she made them as a children's item and sold them at small craft fairs. Her business is customer driven and she started product lines based on what her customers wanted. As her business grew in size, so did the fairs she was asked to attend. Today, in addition to the regular craft fairs she attends, Mary Linda's product is a draw at two annual community fairs and the Woodstock Fair in Woodstock, Connecticut which has a daily patronage of over 200,000 people for four days each on the Labor Day weekend.

Mary Linda is known as "The Frog Lady." Her frogs have won awards as "Best Textile Product." She creates her own templates, traces them onto fabric, sews the two halves together, turns the material and gives her product to me to stuff with polymer beads. She retrieves the stuffed product, adds pompom eyes with black felt pupils and sometimes red felt tongues, adds her personal touch and voila! A new frog, snake or lizard is born.

Mary Linda's frogs, snakes, lizards and turtles have a functional purpose. First, they're for children of all ages: 3 to 103. Next, they are great companions and good luck charms; especially the ones made of sports material. The small frogs, lizards and turtles are pocket pals. The large frogs and lizards are good for door stops. And snakes will fit a standard door and are specifically intended to be used as draft dodgers. However, the sports snakes usually end up on sports bars, are draped over furniture, or end up in vehicles on dash boards or in back windows. There is also a six-foot snake that is made specifically for French doors and sliders.

The Frog Lady has a customer base that looks forward to her returning to their communities each year. Some customers are generational. She has customers who purchased frogs from her when they were children and now they bring their children to the craft fairs. Some of her customers only attend the craft fair to buy a frog and then they go home. Many customers have become friends.

My Friend Mohammad

Mohammad Ahmed arrived in the United States in 1995. He is from Bangladesh. He brought his wife and two young daughters to America to make a better life. Mohammad is a hard worker and he held two jobs. One job was selling vacuum cleaners and the other job was as a bank teller. Today Mohammad is a bank branch manager in Burlington, Massachusetts.

Mohammad earned his U.S. citizenship in 2000 and wanted a driver's license. He studied very hard and aced the written portion of the exam; but failed the driving portion with parallel parking. He failed parking five times. Mohammad told me about his dilemma and I assured him his situation would be rectified.

We met at 7:00 am on a Sunday morning at the Burlington Mall, Burlington, Massachusetts. I tossed him the keys to my new Dodge Intrepid and told him he would learn how to park before the mall opened at 10:00 am. Mohammed practiced for three hours until he literally could have parked blind folded. Although, I really wouldn't want him to do that with my new car.

Mohammad took his sixth and final driving test the following day. He was very happy and proud to finally have a valid driver's license.

My Intrepid served me well until I gave it to my son Dominic a few years ago and bought my truck that doesn't start in the rain.

CIGARETTES & ME

Not counting the corn silk I smoked when I was five years old, I actually started smoking cigarettes when I was crossing the Pacific en-route to South Viet Nam on the U.S.S. General George Weigel. Twenty eight days of lounging on deck, playing cards and smoking cigarettes. It only took one pay check to learn how to play hearts.

Forty years of burn holes in my clothes, little burn specks in the back seats of my cars, and searching for a cigarette or cigarette butt when I ran out. My day would begin with four packs of cigarettes. Two were for me, of which I would smoke half a cigarette and discard the other half. The other two packs were for people who bummed cigarettes from me throughout the day.

At 10:00 am on Sunday, 12 March 2006, I bought four cartons of Marlboro's at the Fort Devens Military Class VI Convenience Store. At 10:00 pm that evening, I was standing outside in the rain smoking a cigarette and said out-loud to myself, "Why am I doing this?" I threw it into the street and haven't touched a cigarette since. Forty years of smoking ended that night. It has now been more than three years without a cigarette.

Max's History Paper

My great nephew Max had to write a paper about Vietnam for his high school history class. I provided information about the history of the country dating back to colonial times; Vietnam's role in World War II; what contributed to the defeat of the French at Dien Bien Phu; and the geopolitical reasons the United States became involved in what amounted to be a civil war.

I also provided information about the initial involvement of U.S. Army Special Forces and its later role in the conflict. Then as the war escalated what the roles of U.S. air and ground forces were. To round out his paper, Max received a couple tidbits about the role played by his great uncle Dave.

Max's high school history paper received an "A."

Circa 2008. September-October time frame. I was approached by a person from my past. We reminisced and then he said that there were some people who were interested in meeting me. He gave me his card and asked that I call him to set up a briefing.

I thought it over for a few weeks and gave him a call. We set a date and time and he gave me directions to his building. The building was located on the edge of a small town, offset in a wooded area from a state highway. He had told me that when I entered the building, the receptionist would be expecting me and would provide me with visitor credentials.

When I arrived, I parked in the parking lot adjacent to the building. It was a nondescript, two story windowless gray building. I knew exactly what it was because at one time I was in charge of a similar $2,000,000.00 building. After signing in and being given my credentials, the receptionist asked me to please be seated in the waiting area. I sat on an overstuffed leather couch and glanced at the magazines on the coffee table. It gave me a chuckle. On the coffee table was the latest issue of GQ Magazine. On the cover was a photo of Kiefer Sutherland. The main article was about Kiefer Sutherland. He was riding a horse and advertising a line of men's western wear.

My friend came out and welcomed me. Then it was a tour of the offices and introductions. He introduced me as a retired Special Forces Command Sergeant Major with a distinguished Military career, etc., etc. I just tagged along. One person suspiciously asked, "Why are you here?" My response was, "Just visiting." This was the Homeland Security element for the state of Massachusetts. The personnel were either Federal Agents or Detectives with the Massachusetts State Police; and Intelligence Analysts in the field of law enforcement and counter-terrorism. The last person I met was in charge of the operation. It's a small world. When he was a young officer in the Reserves, I had taught him rappelling during my first assignment with the 10th Special Forces Group, Fort Devens, Massachusetts.

The briefing I received was quite interesting and informative. After the briefing, I was shown an empty office. The position was new and vacant. It called for someone with a background and experience in

Special Operations and Intelligence to be in charge of what I had just been briefed on. I stated that I was over 60 years old and that life was behind me. My friend responded that he was also over 60 and there wouldn't be any field work involved. It was an Analyst position. He said the opening would be a short window and he would e-mail instructions to me when it became available. A week later, I turned in my resume to the Human Resources Office, Massachusetts State Police Headquarters. Human Resources called me a couple of days later and thanked me for my application, but the position was for an internal opening and not open to the public. I called my friend to let him know and he told me there wasn't anyone qualified to fill the position and when the opening became public, he would e-mail me again.

In the interim, Massachusetts elected a new governor who put a hiring freeze on state positions except for his political appointments. In a way, I'm glad things turned out how they did. And that was my introduction to the politics of Homeland Security.

My simplistic view of the hierarchy of the retail company that currently employs me is to equate leadership positions to Military leadership positions. In my mind, my equation presents an orderly structure to an otherwise confusing line and block chart. The store manager is the First Sergeant. Next are the managers. There are three, four and sometimes five managers in the store, depending on how the wind blows. They have divided among them the various retail, support and service departments. These people are the Platoon Sergeants. Each department has a supervisor whom I equate to being a Squad Leader. Some departments have one or two assistant supervisors whose job title is designated as senior. They do all the work for less pay. In my Military analogy, these people are Assistant Squad Leaders. Then there are the full time and part time employees whom I equate to the rank and file. I belong in this category. We are the Privates.

Miss Kimberly Gilman is one of two seniors in the operations department. The public face of operations is customer service and the cash registers near the exit. Other aspects of operations aren't relevant here. About a year ago, Kim was the only senior in operations and a new person was hired to fill the vacant second position. A part of the senior's duties is to count the receipts at close of business and in essence, to balance the books for the day's receipts. With a new person on board, closing duties were alternately scheduled just in the off chance one or both of the seniors had a life. The new person was still learning the ropes. The operations manager worked daytime hours on the days the new operations senior was scheduled to close. By happenstance, the new person and Kim switched shifts without informing management. Kim performed closing duties on the new person's shift. She noticed a discrepancy in the receipts that only a person with experience would catch. She researched some previous receipts for nights she didn't balance the books. The discrepancies were repeating themselves and they involved thousands of dollars for each day. They were all transactions approved by the store operations manager. Miss Gilman had discovered embezzlement.

There are corporate procedures in place for handling such situations, but this was her boss. Kim didn't know who to trust with the information. She sought advice from a department supervisor that she trusted. He in turn contacted a manager whom he felt was totally trustworthy. Thus, corporate procedures were implemented and Miss Kimberly Gilman was responsible for probably saving the company tens of thousands of dollars.

Periodically, Best Buy undergoes a change which usually involves an internal reorganization. Recently, one of those changes took place and it resulted in the reduction of manager, supervisor and senior leadership positions. Through reviewing performance evaluations, corporate decided who, at the retail store level, would fill the new leadership positions. The operations department was cut one senior position. The person selected to occupy that position was Miss Kimberly Gilman. I believe the correct choice was made.

WAR STORIES

During the 2008 presidential campaign, a candidate misstated facts about her trip to Bosnia. The media jumped all over it, calling her "misspoken" words a war story.

"There I was" is an outlandish fabrication that only the completely gullible will believe. An example used by many a Chairborne Ranger, is: "There I was, knee deep in hand grenade pins...."

War stories describe actual events, usually in the first person. A phenomenon endemic to war stories is that combat soldiers have a tendency to "borrow" each others' war stories. Two guys could be in the same room telling verbatim the same story. Mostly, it's in fun.

The one thing that war story tellers absolutely cannot tolerate is people who lie or fabricate situations when they were nowhere near what was going on. "Misspoken" translated means "lied."

On the flight home from Viet Nam, I was fortunate to be entertained by a young Saigon Warrior (I would say a company clerk by looking at the ink pen sticking out of his neatly starched jungle fatigue pocket and his shoulder insignia for the Third Logistics Command). He was doing his utmost to impress a stewardess about his combat experience. There are also sometimes dubious reasons for telling war stories. The stewardess had asked him why his dog tags were on his boot laces. He was wearing highly shined jungle boots with no sign of ever seeing a rice paddy or the red dirt from Viet Nam that was ground in to every item you owned and every pore on your body. In his bravado combat-experienced voice, he told her the reason was so that his body could be identified if he were killed in action. I tried really hard not to laugh or show even the slightest semblance of a smile. The kid was working hard. I remember thinking how dog tags on boot laces wouldn't work very well in the Mekong Delta with all the booby traps and land mines. When I was with the Seal Team at My Phuoc Tay, we zipped through rice paddies on swamp boats and anti-personnel mines were detonated behind us. (The previous sentence was a "war story." War stories can be a phrase, sentence or paragraph).

During the 2008 presidential campaign, there was only one candidate qualified to tell war stories...and he didn't.

THE DODO

The Dodo was a large flightless bird that lived on the Island of Mauritius in the Indian Ocean and became extinct in the late 17th century. "To go the way of the dodo" is a phrase commonly associated with things that cease to exist.

The following story is about things with which I had an association, and sometimes during that association or when I was no longer associated with them, their function or form ceased to exist. That is the thought process I used to come up with a title for this story. I'm hoping it will meet with James Waddick's approval.

I'll begin with my Army basic combat training. My basic combat training was conducted at Fort Leonard Wood, Missouri. After my graduation, the training regiment to which I was assigned, the 3rd Training Regiment (Basic) was redesignated as the 3rd Basic Combat Training Brigade. It later went through a couple more iterations of being redesignated. First it was redesignated as the 3rd Basic Training Brigade and finally, into the form that it operates under today, the 3rd Combat Training Brigade.

After I was assigned to Viet Nam, the 3rd Special Forces Group at Fort Bragg, North Carolina was inactivated. The weapon I took to Viet Nam, the M-14 Rifle, was useless when I arrived because the Army had switched to the M-16 Rifle and there wasn't any 7.62mm ammunition for the M-14 Rifle in the whole country of South Viet Nam. The 403rd Special Operations Detachment was inactivated and the 5th Special Forces Group was reassigned to Fort Bragg, North Carolina a few months after I left Viet Nam.

The 7th Radio Research Field Station (Ramasun Station) was closed a few years after I left Thailand. I went to Okinawa from Thailand, and while I was on temporary duty in Korea, the 1st Special Forces Group was inactivated. My unit, the 400th Special Operations Detachment, packed up and moved to Fort Bragg, North Carolina and after a short stint with the John F. Kennedy Special Warfare Center, we became a part of the 5th Special Forces Group with a mission focus toward the Middle East.

I went to Iran, trained the Shah's Imperial Guard, met the Shah and returned to Fort Bragg. The Shah was later deposed and Iran wasn't our friend anymore.

During the Carter years, the Army underwent a massive reorganization. Primarily because of funding or a lack there of, belt tightening was in order. Regardless of the reason, some organizations were inactivated and others with similar missions were consolidated. The 400th Special Operations Detachment became a couple iterations of a Combat Tactical Intelligence Company and finally just a Special Forces Military Intelligence Company. The name changed, but the people were the same.

Both units that I ran in Germany were absorbed into larger entities after I left and they no longer exist. When I left the 10th Special Forces Group at Fort Devens and moved across post to the Intelligence School, the 10th Special Forces Group packed up and moved to Fort Carson, Colorado.

When I left the Intelligence School for an assignment in Panama, the Intelligence School packed up and moved to Fort Huachuca, Arizona and Fort Devens was shut down. After I left Panama, my unit was inactivated, the Panama Canal was returned to Panama, and U.S. Army presence was non-existent in Panama.

Most recently, the retail organization I joined a few years ago has undergone an organizational restructure. Best Buy prides itself on diversity and change and is currently operating under a new working model. The current working model in no way resembles the working model I joined three years ago.

And finally, there is Blue Shirt Nation. This online group of people from around the world grew to a membership of over 25,000 Best Buy employees. The site administrators worked diligently to make it better for the employees and for the company. Because of varying time zones, there were nights that I was chatting with new online Blue Shirt Nation friends a half a world away. The Blue Shirt Nation that I joined no longer exists. In the process of upgrading and making it a better site, the instant messaging feature recently disappeared with the advent of a newer and better work and social site...Mix@Blueshirtnation. Now employees can communicate through cell phone messaging, email and online. In addition, Mix is interactive with other corporate sites. Real time live interactions went away. The old is gone and the new is here.

Blue Shirt Nation (BSN) was conceived and brought to life by Best Buy corporate employees Gary Koelling and Steve Bendt in February 2007. The original thought was to use BSN as a means of getting advertising feedback from Best Buy retail store employees.

What the founders found out was that Blue Shirt Nation was a vehicle for work and social networking by rank and file employees who were passionate about the company and wanted to make it better. One significant result was that Blue Shirt Nation directly contributed to increased employee retention and employee participation in the Best Buy 401K retirement plan.

Membership in this online phenomenon included corporate executives and employees, and management and employees in the field. In July 2007, I became BSN member number 8112. By the end of 2008, Blue Shirt Nation had grown to 25,000 employees in a 100,000 employee company. Blue Shirt Nation became a voice for the rank and file. This was quite evident in late 2007 when a new corporate policy was to be implemented that directly affected employees. There were hundreds of online discussions about the intended policy change and the feeling in the field was that the policy was not a good thing. The corporate response was "we hear you loud and clear" and the new policy wasn't implemented.

Best Buy as an entity prides itself on transparency. Policies and business practices put into place are there to benefit its customers, employees and stockholders. It is a fun place to work.

In the beginning, there were members of Blue Shirt Nation who were a driving force for this entity to grow. One such person was Miss Ashley Hemsath. Her online persona was "Malicat." The avatar she used to represent herself online was a Calico kitten. She described herself on her home page with "I AM BEST BUY."

Malicat was bright and intelligent. She had innovative ideas for helping Best Buy. She wanted the company to grow and succeed.

In late 2007 a series of tragic events happened in Ashley's life that were overwhelming. Condolences from her online friends were all that we could offer. Rather than not be a positive force in Best Buy and on Blue Shirt Nation, Miss Ashley Hemsath tendered a from the heart letter of resignation. She is sorely missed.

Blue Shirt Nation has been the conduit for employees from around the world to communicate and exchange ideas for good and sound business practices. It has also been a place for making new friends. There were many nights in 2007 and 2008 when I was instant messaging with Best Buy online friends from coast to coast; and in Alaska, Hawaii and Canada. I talked business with one friend while he was vacationing with his family in Cancun Mexico.

Groups were formed to communicate like ideas. I belong to 40 groups and formed two groups myself…one for appliances and one for Military. There are many Military affiliations in Best Buy and the Military Group was the place for people to discuss issues regarding deployments, housing, and where to go to get answers to questions.

In late 2008, the new and improved Blue Shirt Nation was born. It became Mix. The home page says it all: "Mix is a service for Best Buy employees who want to stay connected via email, sms, or web. Stay connected…Share and access information anytime anywhere. Share stuff. Collaborate…Mix connects us and makes us more valuable to each other and our customers."

Friendships I have made through Blue Shirt Nation and Mix will last me a life time. Blue Shirt Nation was ground breaking in the business world and its inception and success are due to the perseverance of two men who had an innovative idea and wanted to make a difference.

It is fitting that I end this with what has come to be my online entry signature:

I'm done.

This is the end of my book. As I write this, I have only completed about one-third of the manuscript. But, this story may be an appropriate ending. Since you the reader are on this page, you know I had an adventurous childhood, a personally rewarding Military career, and a quiet retirement. And the past few years, I have been employed with Best Buy, Inc.; a fun place to work.

Prior to beginning the business day, management has a morning meeting with associates that has some form of ice breaker. Late last fall, one ice breaker was a game of flag Nerf football behind the store. Two managers were team captains and they selected their teams. As selections progressed, it came down to two people. The eighty-eight pound media girl and me, the 60-ish old guy. The media girl was picked.

Fast forward to the present. There was a program about gang warfare on the TV in the break room. Two managers were talking about forming their own gangs. One manager said, "I'll go first. I pick Dave Carden." And finally, I recently attended a company evening training session. During a break, people were discussing an upcoming company sponsored event at a paint ball arena. One of the sales people from another department said, "I want Dave Carden on my team."

EPILOGUE

It's been a good run. I lived the childhood of a lifetime, was blessed with a loving and wonderful family, was afforded the opportunity to honorably serve my country, blessed again with a beautiful wife and four great children, once again blessed with beautiful grandchildren, and am now enjoying retirement in a quiet little town with the person with whom I'll spend the rest of my life.

I am now entering the twilight years. The average lifespan today is 75 years. As I said before, it's been a good run.

DAVID C. CARDEN
Sergeant Major, U.S. Army (Retired)
Summer 2009